Get Your Church Ready to Grow

A Guide to Building Attendance and Participation

John Zehring

JUDSON PRESS
PUBLISHERS SINCE 1824
VALLEY FORGE, PA

Interior design by Beth Oberholtzer.
Cover design by Wendy Ronga, Hampton Design Group.

Library of Congress Cataloging-in-Publication data

Names: Zehring, John William, author.
Title: Get your church ready to grow / John Zehring.
Description: First [edition]. | Valley Forge : Judson Press, 2018.
Identifiers: LCCN 2017025705 | ISBN 9780817017910 (pbk. : alk. paper)
Subjects: LCSH: Church growth.
Classification: LCC BV652.25 .Z44 2018 | DDC 254/.5--dc23 LC record
    available at https://lccn.loc.gov/2017025705

Printed in the U.S.A.

First printing, 2018.

Contents

Introduction

Most churches want to grow. Every church would love to see young families and new members streaming in the door. "We must be doing something right," we say when attendance rises. Numerical growth feels good, fuels the budget, and staffs the volunteer needs of the choir, educational programs, and committees. When attendance declines, we say, "We must be doing something wrong." We think that maybe we need to get a new pastor, change our music, or advertise in the newspaper or online. Therein lies a theological conundrum: attendance is linked to feelings, mood, morale, and a confirmation that something is either right or wrong.

Your attendance growth or decline is more likely linked to the demographic shifts of your zip code than to anything else. If your zip code is growing 10 percent per year, you will likely see a growth spurt in church attendance even if you are flubbing everything you can. On the other hand, if your zip code is shrinking 10 percent per year, you will likely see a decline in church attendance, even if you produce the most Spirit-filled, vibrant, and inspiring worship services ever created. So, begin with the reality that much of growth or decline is linked to demographics. And culture. If the culture reflects a decline in membership-based organizations (churches, country clubs, teams, museums, etc.), recognize that good programming alone will not swim against the strong tide of the culture's inclination to avoid the commitment of belonging to an organization.

Congregations that have experienced long-term steady growth in attendance and participation testify to three realities:

1. *There is no magic bullet.* There is no canned dog-and-pony show program, no quick fix, no "if only you do this you will grow," no magic ingredient, no secret that megachurches know that you do not, no quick formulas, and no single solution to stemming decline and increasing attendance. The answer lies in doing many things. Some, like a balanced investment portfolio, will be more effective than others, but together they contribute to growth. Quit your search for the Holy Grail of building attendance. That would be like searching for a single stock in which to invest. Rather, do many things simultaneously.

2. *Building attendance growth takes a long time.* Church leaders or members may look for quick results and solutions that lead to instant gratification. That can be a frustration to wise pastoral leadership that knows that growth is measured over a period of years and not Sunday to Sunday. Slow progress is fine. Studies of growing churches like those conducted by the Hartford Institute for Religion Research typically state growth in terms of "grew 2 percent or more in the past five years." Remember, progress is always to be preferred over regress. A church may need to work three to five years on building attendance and participation before the "breakout" occurs and the growth spurt makes a significantly noticeable leap. Congregations that build attendance determine that they truly desire to grow and then work at it over and over again for years. Trust no one who promises fast results.

3. *Building attendance and participation requires investment of financial resources and time, leadership skills, the shifting of volunteer assets from one priority to another, and staff commitment and energy.* It cannot happen without investment. Growth can be costly, although not as costly as decline. If growth in attendance and participation is envisioned for self-serving purposes, there may be little impetus for significant investment. On the other hand, if growth is envisioned for the theological purpose of meeting the spiritual needs of more people in your community, it becomes a mission, min-

istry, and outreach of the church, which has the potential to inspire increased financial support and a worthy investment of time and energy. Consequently, the metaphor featured in *Get Your Church Ready to Grow* is taken from the world of investments, risk, portfolio, and action based on research rather than gut instinct or uninformed opinion.

A former parishioner and beloved friend called me one day. He was now living in Florida, and his small church in a community of the elderly was floundering and declining and was threatened with extinction. He innocently asked me for my opinion about a quick fix or magical solution to propel them into quick and hearty growth. I wish I had such a fix, but aspiring to build attendance and participation requires investment and shifting of priorities. His was an extreme case but illustrated for me the need for the quiz that follows to help congregations determine their readiness for growth. Take the quiz for your church. Have others take it too, and share results with one another. Wherever a church falls on the readiness scale, there are steps you can take to help build attendance and participation. You will find help to discern a direction to take into the future and some ideas and actions to employ that will get you where you want to be.

If you want to grow your church, you will need to invest. Think about your personal savings and investments. How do you decide what to invest in? Your best decisions will be based on the wisdom of experienced advisers, on self-education about investments that could accomplish your goals, and on the likely consequences of your investments. And so Part 3 provides guidance on how to base your church's time, energy, and investment in growth on data by using a congregational survey, focus groups, and exit information from those who have left or are leaving the church. Allow the data to guide your investment rather than relying on hunches, opinions, and guesses when a few well-placed actions may suffice in the same way that a few well-chosen index funds may balance your financial portfolio, protecting you in downturns and allowing you to take advantage of up times.

The number one ingredient to growing church attendance and participation is the *desire* to grow. Instill that desire in congregational leaders, and encourage them to own that goal and to recognize that the *motivation* to build attendance and participation is a hundred times more important than whatever method is used to achieve that goal. A congregation that desires to grow will invest energy and resources to accomplish their goal. Name the goal, embrace the goal, own the goal, and pursue the goal.

Growth in *Get Your Church Ready to Grow* is equated with building attendance and participation, not with membership growth. We live in an age and culture where people's interest in membership is in decline, even though they will pick and choose to attend or participate in selected pieces and parts of your church's ministry. *Growth* in this book is not about boosting membership rolls, although they may benefit. It is somewhat about filling seats at worship. Mostly it is about your church meeting needs through a variety of experiences that attract people even if they attend worship infrequently. They might attend a small-group ministry or participate in a short-term adult education unit even if you do not see them Sunday after Sunday. The goal is to meet spiritual needs where and how you find them, to touch lives, to let people know the church is there for them, and to count the lives you've touched, affected, and served rather than simply adding to the numbers on your membership rolls.

Here is a delightful consequence of actions to grow your church: if your church engages with enthusiasm in even a portion of ideas and actions to build attendance and participation, the swirl of activity alone will launch energy and excitement that will encourage members to bring in friends, neighbors, and family. Let your members see that your leaders and staff clearly desire for your church to reach out to meet the spiritual needs of more people in your community. Then the swirl of activity will spiral upward and outward so that meeting needs becomes one of the congregation's primary focus points and celebration activities. Energy begets energy. The contagion spreads, and all members pool their wisdom and resources to support the congregation's mission to meet the needs of more people in your community.

Myths about Building Church Attendance

Consider some myths about how to build church attendance.

"If you build it, they will come."

That's a line from Hollywood. "Build a better mousetrap, and the world will beat a path to your door," noted Ralph Waldo Emerson in the 1800s when that might have worked. Not today. Of course, build the best worship service and program you possibly can. Build a faithful congregation.

God does not call your church to be successful. God calls your church to be faithful. People today are seeking a center for spiritual renewal where their spirits can be renewed, their minds can be challenged, their souls can find comfort, and their energies can be tapped for important and meaningful service to others. Build a worship service that responds to the needs of those who are seeking. However, simply doing more of the same or even improving your already excellent program will not build church attendance. You might think that it will, but it will not. Inspired preaching, uplifting music, and a multifaceted program alone will not build attendance, although the absence of these will contribute to decline.

"We can get it for free or next to nothing."

Your church is already hurting financially. All churches are. That is not necessarily bad: if your congregation has more than it needs, that means it is not giving away enough to help others. But even financially strapped congregations can find the resources to support what is most important to them. And after all, the truth always stares us in the face: you get what you pay for.

For example, a congregation desired earnestly to develop a strong youth program. It was their fervent belief that a strong youth program was (a) part of what God was calling them to do and (b) a worthy investment in the future of the body of Christ. Most youth programs in the community were failing or were nonexistent. So, they decided to put their money where their heart was: they took a huge leap of faith and invested financially in a full-time youth director. At first not much changed. A year later the program jelled and the youth of the church came regularly, some bringing friends. The following year more youth came in from the outside; a mission trip attracted many, and programming for youth mushroomed. Then the growth spurt continued, grew, and finally produced satisfying results: a full-blown, highly active, vital, and attractive youth program that outperformed all early expectations. Their investment paid off and yielded the goal they planned.

A thousand other stories will tell of desires for the same outcome but with no investment. If you want results, you must invest. It is not free, and to do it cheap produces cheap results. Likewise with building attendance and membership growth in churches. Invest seriously if you want significant results. Investing to build attendance has the potential to recoup some of or even surpass all of the investment.

"If people would only bring a friend, we would grow."

The number one factor for attendance growth has been and always will be word-of-mouth advertising. When one person says to another, "Will you come with me on Sunday?" that guest is likely to come and then to come back and remain.

Consider the range of word-of-mouth invitations. On the one hand, to tell a friend how much you enjoy your church and how it meets your spiritual needs is highly significant. On the other hand, to invite a person to come with you, even to offer to pick them up, sit with them, and introduce them to people afterward has an off-the-scale success rate. Bring-a-Friend Sundays inspire members to consider the value of their own testimony and invitation to friends. But in reality, where are the long-term results? The challenge is to sustain this kind of effort on a weekly basis, and that does not appear to be happening in most congregations.

"We must grow to achieve our budget."

Potential attendees can smell self-serving reasons for building attendance from a thousand paces away. "We can't afford our pastor's salary unless we replenish the members who are moving way, leaving, or dying." "It's becoming harder to recruit committee members." "We can never attract enough church school teachers." "Our choir is growing older and shrinking."

The moment you become primarily self-serving about building attendance and participation, your theological base weakens. Building attendance as a ministry to meet the spiritual needs of others can excite the enthusiasm of many members. Simply working to attract more people to sustain the institution has a less compelling appeal. Your worries about your church budget and shrinking volunteer pool are real, but if all you are looking for are warm bodies and deep pockets, you will repel potential participants in your community of faith. You can smell it, you can feel it in the air, and you can hear it plainly. What visitors will hear is: *"How can we use you?"* What they need to hear is, *"How can we serve you? How can we come alongside you?"*

Reasons to Grow

Balance the church's need to increase attendance and participation with your altruistic outreach to meet the needs of others. Frame your campaign theologically: *to meet needs. Their needs.* The moment you shift your attention to meeting their needs, you become spiritually centered in offering that which you possess in service to another. Is that not a definition of ministry?

The epicenter of building attendance and participation revolves around the Godlike attitude of wanting to meet the needs of others. Start by affirming that your church meets needs. Your congregation meets the spiritual needs of participants better than any other human organization. Your church meets the holistic needs of a person and recognizes that a person cannot be whole without God in his or her life. When a person is not whole, he or she is fragmented. For people whose lives feel fragmented, your church offers a pathway to becoming whole. The key question becomes: "How many more needs of people can we meet?" Is it possible that you could meet the needs of another fifty people? One hundred people? Two hundred?

How do you address this question? Begin by counting the seats in your sanctuary. Then estimate a year-round average attendance. In general, weekly attendance averages about 40 to 50 percent of the membership. Or count how many empty seats you have on average. Suppose you have a sanctuary that can accommodate 300 worshippers but your average attendance is 120. You have, on average, room for 180 more. If you met the needs of 180 new attenders, could you accommodate them and assimilate them into the life of your congregation?

Do not obsess over numbers, but neither be afraid to set some numerical goals. Suppose, for example, that you determined that you could meet the needs of another one hundred people. Suppose, in addition, that you stated that you would like to attain that goal within five years. Seeking to attract an additional twenty people a year for five years is doable. Naming a goal keeps the motivation to build attendance continually before leaders and members of the congregation and inspires strategic planning to achieve the goal. Never underestimate the skills and motivation of your leaders to (1) state a goal, (2) create a plan to meet the goal, (3) reevaluate along the way progress toward achieving the goal, and (4) shift resources and assets to accomplish the goal.

To put this in theological language, *people are lost and God wants them found.* Or, *people are seeking and you know in your heart that your church meets needs.* Choose the right reasons to grow, recognize the realities about how this can take a long time, and pursue many strategies simultaneously. The alternative: decline.

In Jesus' parable of the sower, note that only 25 percent of the seeds yielded results. Jesus explained the reasons why the others did not, but consider his batting average: .250. Nobody bats a thousand. Neither will you. Your job is to plant the seed. It is God who gives growth. Even then some seeds will blow away with the wind, others will grow up but be choked out by weeds, and still others will sprout roots but eventually wither. Only a portion will take root and produce fruit. Even in Jesus' experience, crowds witnessed his teaching but few followed.

And so, with patience and hope, we plant trees under whose shade we may never sit. Yet God reaps the harvest from our sowing. You are not accountable for the reaping—just the sowing. You never know the effect the seed is having. You might be surprised to know the helpful impact you make from things you have said or done. The harvest is sure. In spite of the lost effort on the path and among the rocks and the thorns, some harvest will come. It always will. The harvest is sure because God's Word is powerful. When God's truth is spoken, a portion of the audience will have ears to hear, and the Word will take root, grow, and bear fruit in this portion. This is the most encouraging message from the parable of the sower: the harvest is sure.

"If you build it, they will come." Some will anyway.

Get Your Church Ready to Grow does not present a one-size-fits-all strategic plan but instead provides a multitude of possible investments for you to draw from as you create a portfolio to meet the spiritual needs of more people and build attendance and participation in your church.

May God inspire, bless, and nurture your efforts to meet the needs of others who are hungering for what you have found. You are planting the seeds of the kingdom of God.

The Parable of the Sower
(Matthew 13:1-9,18-23)

That same day Jesus went out of the house and sat beside the sea. Such great crowds gathered around him that he got into a boat and sat there, while the whole crowd stood on the beach. And he told them many things in parables, saying: "Listen! A sower went out to sow. And as he sowed, some seeds fell on the path, and the birds came and ate them up. Other seeds fell on rocky ground, where they did not have much soil, and they sprang up quickly, since they had no depth of soil. But when the sun rose, they were scorched; and since they had no root, they withered away. Other seeds fell among thorns, and the thorns grew up and choked them. Other seeds fell on good soil and brought forth grain, some a hundredfold, some sixty, some thirty. Let anyone with ears listen!". . .

"Hear then the parable of the sower. When anyone hears the word of the kingdom and does not understand it, the evil one comes and snatches away what is sown in the heart; this is what was sown on the path. As for what was sown on rocky ground, this is the one who hears the word and immediately receives it with joy; yet such a person has no root, but endures only for a while, and when trouble or persecution arises on account of the word, that person immediately falls away. As for what was sown among thorns, this is the one who hears the word, but the cares of the world and the lure of wealth choke the word, and it yields nothing. But as for what was sown on good soil, this is the one who hears the word and understands it, who indeed bears fruit and yields, in one case a hundredfold, in another sixty, and in another thirty."

Ready to Grow?
Readiness for Growth* Quiz

*Growth = in this context, increased attendance and participation

1. Rate the population growth or decline of your town, village, or city:
    a. Growing fast
    b Growing some
    c. Staying about the same
    d. Declining

2. Estimate your pastor's interest in growing the church:
    a. Very high
    b. High
    c. Some interest
    d. Not interested

3. Estimate the interest of your church's leaders in growing the church:
    a. Very high
    b. High
    c. Some interest
    d. Not interested

4. What is your church's primary motivation for growth?
    a. Meet spiritual needs of more people
    b. Build a stronger future for the church
    c. Need more money, volunteers, teachers, choir members
    d. Not interested in growth

5. How willing is your church to invest financially to seek growth?
    a. Ready to raise or borrow funds to invest in growth
    b. Willing to try to find some new resources for growth
    c. Could reshuffle some resources to seek growth
    d. Not willing or able to invest anything

6. How willing is your church to revise the pastor's job description to make growth a high priority? (This means some things have to go or be done by lay members)
    a. Willing to eliminate some major responsibilities to free pastor to pursue growth
    b. Willing to eliminate some minor responsibilities to free pastor to pursue growth
    c. Willing to add growth to job description but not at the expense of removing anything
    d. Not willing to change the job description

7. How willing is your church to hire additional staff (music, education, nursery, youth, pastoral) to attract higher rates of attendance and participation?
    a. Ready to add one or more full-time staff to facilitate building attendance and participation
    b. Might consider a part-time or contract addition but not willing or able to invest in full-time or multiple hires
    c. Could reorganize current responsibilities but not add staff
    d. No resources for new staff, and current staff are too busy to ask them to add one more thing

8. MUSIC: How willing is your current staff to make changes in the music program to provide more opportunities for participation and to meet a wider range of musical tastes?
   a. High interest, especially if doing so would make a way to accomplish goals
   b. Some interest, but only with additional staffing
   c. Little interest. Would need pastoral or congregational mandate to redirect goals of the program
   d. No interest. People prefer our existing program.

9. EDUCATION: How willing is your current staff to increase engagement, encourage teachers, and introduce innovations toward a goal of attracting new participants and increasing attendance?
   a. Energized by the challenge and highly supportive, especially if it can accomplish the goal
   b. Some interest, but only with additional staffing
   c. Little interest. Would need pastoral or congregational mandate to redirect goals of the program
   d. No interest. People like our program the way it is; no need to create new ministries of education

10. COMMUNICATIONS: How willing is your congregation to invest in changes to your church's communications strategy (website, newsletter, worship bulletin, social media) to attract new people and engage increased participation?
   a. Eager to explore technologies and strategies to be attractive, responsive to guest and visitor needs, and enthusiastic about emphasizing opportunities for programs, ministry, and service
   b. Would like to upgrade our website and be more creative, but we lack the skill sets or the funds for more than routine maintenance
   c. Focus on basic information for members and interested visitors; doing the best we can with the time and resources we have.
   d. No need for bells and whistles to say who we are

11. WORSHIP: How would you rate the importance and value of weekly worship in your church and in the life of the congregation?

    a. Top priority of our staff and leaders. Designed to lead people into an encounter with the divine through coordinated music, liturgy, and preaching; services have high involvement of laity, youth, and children

    b. Very important. Staff members do their best to create a service that fosters a time for the church community to worship and fellowship together

    c. Some services are more worshipful than others; you cannot meet everyone's needs, of course, and some people do not like various aspects of the service

    d. A cure for insomnia; needs work

12. UPON ENTERING THE CHURCH: How effective is your church in welcoming members and guests alike?

    a. Trained greeters welcome those entering and try to introduce visitors to the pastor or other leaders; first-time attenders get an information packet about the church; helpful signs direct people to the sanctuary, classrooms, and restrooms; accessible entrances are provided and clearly marked

    b. Greeters, though untrained, welcome in a friendly manner and hand out bulletins; no visitor packets, but a church brochure is available on a rack nearby; there are a few signs, but guests can ask ushers for directions

    c. When people enter the sanctuary, an usher will give them a bulletin and show them to a seat; no signs to direct first attenders, and restrooms are hard to find; no special access for those with mobility challenges

    d. An aging congregation without resources, but happy to wish members and the rare visitor a warm welcome

SCORING

of a's: _____ x 4 = _____
# of b's: _____ x 3 = _____
# of c's: _____ x 2 = _____
# of d's: _____ x 1 = _____
SCORE: _____

RESULTS (48 maximum)

40+ High readiness, high investment, and already doing much. Use ideas to strengthen your efforts. Congratulations for being a model of desiring to meet needs.

30 to 40 Moderate readiness, already doing some. You have the greatest capacity to leap forward with increased investment and encouragement to leaders and staff. You may have the most to gain by ideas in this book. You are well-poised to meet the needs of more people in your community.

20 to 30 Potential readiness. More conversation, prayer, and planning are needed among church leaders and staff. Pluck the low-hanging fruit. Align expectations with the church's investment of time, energy, goals, and resources. Consider a long-range plan toward growth, and begin taking one step at a time.

0 to 20 Low readiness to grow. Learn to be content with who you are and what you have, as the apostle Paul wrote: "I have learned to be content with whatever I have" (Philippians 4:11). Focus on spiritual growth of those entrusted to you, however few. Reframe your church's self-image to see through lenses of abundance rather than through lenses of scarcity. Talk up your strengths and the needs you meet.

USES

You could ask a hundred different questions, but this dozen gives a quick view of your church's readiness to set building attendance and participation as a priority goal.

Use the quiz as a discussion starter with staff, groups interested in growth, governing boards, and committees. Have each participant score her or his quiz and then discuss among participants your similarities and differences. See if there is a general consensus about your church falling into one of the above categories. Or might there be differences between staff and leaders, or based on ages, educational levels, intensity of participation in the church, or other factors? What if, for example, you discovered that the staff thought the leaders did not have a high interest in growth when in fact they do? Or what if you discovered that perhaps the staff have a high interest only to find that leaders do not? Be clear that there is no judgment involved in sharing results. Instead, invite respondents to use this quiz as a tool to help start a discussion about your church's readiness to grow in building attendance and participation.

Chapter 1
Planning and Preliminary Actions

Get the Staff on Board

Is your church staff overworked, underpaid, and saturated with more responsibilities than can be done well? Increasing attendance may rank twenty-first on their list of the top twenty things they must accomplish on a daily basis. And so if nothing changes, then nothing will change.

One way for the congregation to declare that meeting the needs of more people is a high church priority is for the governing board to affirm this priority for the pastor, with the understanding that other parts of the ministry must be shared or lowered on the scale of priorities. If the pastor, music staff, education staff, and office staff catch the enthusiasm of meeting more needs and seeking to increase participation, their support will undergird the congregation's goal. The staff is vital to increasing attendance. Without the investment of staff's energy, creativity, time, and leadership, not much is likely to change.

Achieving the goal of increasing attendance requires investment. Invest to free staff to devote time to growing the church or add more staff. Simply adding one more thing to the staff's already long laundry list of responsibilities without making possible their freedom to attend to the goal has a high likelihood of being short-lived. Be patient and careful to guide the staff to see the theological reasons for growing the church. Never presume the staff will agree with the goal. Some may be suspicious of why the church should want to grow, perhaps thinking it is for self-aggrandizement reasons. Others may hold the "that's not my job" attitude. Involve all of the staff in all aspects of planning, build an *espirit de corps* attitude, and help the staff to adopt a group goal of desiring to meet the needs of more people.

Get the Laity on Board

The number one factor in building attendance is having your lay members involved in recruiting new people. The more a congregation's laity is involved in recruitment, the more likely growth will happen. A Hartford Institute for Religion Research study published as "American Congregations 2015: Thriving and Surviving"[1] showed that the effect of the laity is dramatic. However, the study found that only 14 percent of congregations say their laity are "quite" or "very involved" in recruitment. The report noted, "Laity's willingness to get involved, this suggests, is one of the key reality checks in any congregational growth strategy."[2] Consider the results: Of the congregations in America that grew 2 percent or more in the past five years, 90 percent of growing churches said there was a lot of involvement by laity. Hence, one of the first steps to growing your church and building attendance is to secure the ownership of the goal by laity. Involve laity in the dreaming, planning, voting, budgeting, and implementing of the goal to meet the needs of more people in your community.

Establish a Culture of Excellence

A church administrator said about her church: "We just scrounge for everything." The appearance of the building bore evidence to what she spoke: offices that looked like storerooms, broken-down furniture, computers from bygone ages, cheaply done publications, dank basement classrooms, grimy bathrooms with no doors on the stalls, hallways cluttered with unused furniture, yellowing artwork on the walls, hand-scribbled signs, bulletin boards from the twentieth century, a narthex cluttered with outdated papers and brochures, out-of-tune pianos with sticking keys, worn and faded pew cushions, and broken toys in the nursery.

Guess what that signals to guests? Answer: *We do not take ourselves seriously. We do not take our faith seriously. We do not take our mission seriously. Excellence is for others. We settle for used-up, worn, and substandard.* That is hardly an attractive outreach to meet needs and build attendance. It reveals that the church is second-rate.

Start to change this unsatisfactory culture by proclaiming that you will take your cue from Paul's counsel to the Philippian church: "Finally, beloved, whatever is true, whatever is honorable, whatever is just, whatever is pure, whatever is pleasing, whatever is commendable, if there is any excellence and if there is anything worthy of praise, think about these things" (4:8). "If there is any *excellence.* . . ." Create a culture of excellence. Work with staff and leaders to adopt an attitude of excellence in all things. Present an environment that shows that you take yourself, your church, and your faith seriously.

There is a saying in business: "First-rate people hire first-rate people. Second-rate people hire third-rate people." Project a first-rate welcome to people who are seeking a center for spiritual renewal. Change the culture to excellence.

A travel expert was instructing people on what to look for in selecting lodging when they travel. She shared a universal truth when she told them, "Hospitality flows from the top down." If you call for information and are not greeted with friendly and helpful assistance, she said, you can assume that the management of the facility does not promote excellence and customer service. Go somewhere else. On the other hand, if at every turn the workers exude a cheerful desire to be as helpful as possible, you can assume that excellence in hospitality is flowing from the top down. So, too, with the church. The pastor, professional staff, and senior volunteer leaders are well-served to embrace and promote a culture of excellence and "customer service." Even though most may not see the leader's hand in it, savvy attenders will suspect that excellence flows from the top down.

Attend to the 80/20 Rule

Eighty percent of the results come from 20 percent of the effort. This is a classic business rule. It even has a name: the Pareto principle. It is also known as the 80/20 rule. Eighty percent of the money comes from 20 percent of the people. Eighty percent of the problems come from 20 percent of the customers. Eighty percent of the sales come from 20 percent of the clients. Eighty percent of the leadership comes from 20 percent of the people. With any major undertaking, such as setting out to meet the spiritual needs of more people in your community and increasing your attendance, 80 percent of the results will derive from 20 percent of your efforts. Therefore, choose wisely how you will invest human and financial capital to accomplish your goal.

For example, if adding one more adult education program brings in roughly the same small group of people who have been attending adult education programs, one more offering does not contribute substantially to meeting the spiritual needs of more people (although it enriches the quality of the program for those being served). On the other hand, if adding a choral ensemble, additional worship opportunity, or small-groups ministry program brings in more new people from the outside, that is a worthy investment. Spend your resources and assets where they will accomplish the most, giving you a higher "return on investment."

Compare two examples: Church A created a concert series with five concerts. It involved a dozen members in planning, publicity, communication with musicians, hospitality and refreshments, and setting up and cleaning up at each concert. Their hope was to attract more people from the community to set foot inside the meetinghouse, which happened. Newspaper and radio announcements about the concerts increased the church's name recognition to thousands. All were enriched by the program, and compliments flowed graciously. Months afterward they discovered that the ambitious undertaking did not yield even one new member or attender at worship. Was it worth it? Absolutely, in terms of enjoyment of the music. It made no impact, however, in building attendance or growing the church.

In contrast, Church B spent six months preparing to overhaul their website. They brought in advisors from their denomination, studied dozens of websites of other congregations, and hired a consultant to help them make their new website attractive, compelling, user-friendly, and oriented especially to those outside the church who were seeking information about the church. The result? Most active members looked at it once or twice and consulted it occasionally for ongoing news and information. However, church shoppers and new attenders dribbled in, a few at first and then more and more over the following years. Then surveys and focus groups asked new people what drew them to participate in the life of the church. The top reason was a personal invitation. The second was the website. Today the website is a top source of information and attraction for reaching new people.

Now apply the 80/20 rule. In terms of yielding results for the goal of building attendance, which efforts made the most difference—Church A or Church B? The answer is obvious although both churches created something good. The point is to focus like a laser beam on the goal you want to achieve and invest efforts to reach that goal.

Put It on the Five-Year Plan

As you set out to meet the spiritual needs of more people in your community, you will be well-served to think in terms of a multiple-year strategic plan. As leaders and staff brainstorm, plan, budget, and implement the plan, it is liberating to know that some objectives are better set in the third, fourth, or fifth year. Everything does not need to be accomplished in one year. Indeed, growing your church may become a lifelong priority rather than a short-lived campaign. Map out a timetable spread over time to balance energy, enthusiasm, and resources.

For example, imagine a year of planning to create a five-year plan. If five ingredients to building attendance were attempted each year, that would yield twenty-five ingredients to building your church over the five years. Then, perhaps, the following year might be spent in evaluation and planning for the next five-year plan.

Turn to Your Denominational Leaders for Consultation

Some denominations have staff members available who specialize in church vitality and growth. If possible, invite the expert to meet with church leaders. Have the pastor take the denominational resource person to lunch. Ask the expert what has worked in your region. Attend church vitality workshops offered by your denomination. You will discover a long list of what has failed. Your objective is to uncover what has yielded results.

Your denominational resource also knows which congregations in your state or region are growing or are experimenting with ideas that hold promise. Ask them who the leaders are and then go visit those people. Make it a field trip for interested leaders to meet with others who can help guide you and save you wasted effort or expense. Do not envy their success but learn from it to see if there is anything that can be applied to your experience.

You may find that your denominational leaders are as interested in growing churches and building attendance as you are. A congregation that sets growth as a high priority and intentionally invests time, wisdom, and funds to meet the needs of more people in their community is rare. Your denominational leaders may take your church under their wing, focus attention on you, use you as a model, and tell others about your efforts. They can link you with other congregations who share your mission and goal. Never underestimate the power of collaboration in discovering creative possibilities by working with others.

Manage Conflict

Conflict within the church is the number one inhibitor to growth. The "American Congregations 2015" study found that 54 percent of congregations that grew 2 percent or more in the past five years reported some conflict but not serious conflict. Only 29 percent of churches that reported serious conflict grew. The report stated:

> Like most people, congregations prefer to avoid conflict, and in fact, are not very good at dealing with it. We have known for some time now that conflict can be a major obstacle to growth. [The study] shows that this remains true. . . . But the [study] also hints at an important nuance. Namely that it is serious conflict that is the real culprit. Indeed, the data show that congregations with no conflict are a bit less likely to grow than those with some, but not serious conflict. Growth will likely cause some tension or conflict. It is being able to keep it from degenerating into serious conflict that is the key.[3]

Conflict is the number one inhibitor to growing your church and building attendance. But conflict is a natural part of life. Therefore the antidote is not to *avoid* conflict but to *manage* it. A congregation that can name its conflict, put it in context, and employ good tools for conflict resolution will be the healthiest and the best candidate for growth. Teach your people not to fear conflict. Educate the congregation to appreciate and embrace a wide diversity of opinions. Encourage members to learn to abide with differing views and to debate them but not to attack persons. Conflict can be managed.

When members become assured that healthy disagreements are nothing to fear, they will enjoy a widespread acceptance of one another. If necessary, get help from outside—perhaps from your denomination's experts or from a consultant—but let the help serve not to solve your problems but to equip the church with tools and skills to resolve and manage conflict in healthy ways. Here is a challenge: the church is a volunteer organization, and volunteer leaders change regularly. Therefore, the educational task of teaching leaders to manage conflict must be repeated over and over as new leaders come on board. Make this a priority and you can reduce the number one inhibitor to building attendance.

Avoid Offending People Who Return after Long Absences

A young family returning to worship after a long time away was greeted at the entrance sidewalk by a faithful regular member who said to them, "Look who's coming to church today! Oh my, the walls of the church may come tumbling down." The young family heard the faux welcome, was duly offended, turned 180 degrees, walked away from the church, and never returned. How many have been lost because of the best intentions of members greeting them with a poor choice of words? Teach your members to be oriented to welcoming all, from first-time attenders to lapsed attenders.

When Abraham Lincoln was asked how he would treat the rebellious Southerners who had left the union and then returned, the questioner expected that Lincoln would require vengeance. Just the opposite. Lincoln answered, "I will treat them as if they had never been away." Grow that kind of spiritual maturity among regular members so that when people come back to church after a lengthy absence, the regular members treat them as if they had never been away. Otherwise everyone loses.

Plant and Pray

Jesus' parable of the sower reminds that we plant, but it is God who gives growth. If your church desires to meet the spiritual needs of more people in your community, pray that the Holy Spirit might lead them to you. Even if many are not interested in organized religion, some are. As people of faith, we believe that human beings possess some kind of spiritual longing: "When he saw the crowds, he had compassion for them, because they were harassed and help-less, like sheep without a shepherd. Then he said to his disciples, 'The harvest is plentiful, but the laborers are few; therefore ask the Lord of the harvest to send out laborers into his harvest'" (Matthew 9:36-38).

You know that your church meets spiritual needs. Many have testified so. Build a campaign to request your members to pray that God will guide those with needs to you. Invite your people to pray for growth in worship, in committees and boards, in staff meetings, and in their personal prayers. Keep growth on their radar screen. Encourage your people to pray not so much for the church's gain but for the people's needs. Ask the Lord of the harvest to send out laborers into his harvest that people may see your good works and give glory to God.

NOTES

1. David A. Roozen, "American Congregations 2015: Thriving and Surviving," Hartford Institute for Religion Research, accessed January 12, 2018, http://hirr.hartsem.edu/American-Congregations-2015.pdf.

2. Ibid., 5.

3. Ibid.

Chapter 2
Educating and Informing Yourself

As you work to grow the attendance of your church, learn to accept with serenity the things that cannot be changed. The Hartford Institute for Religion Research's study "American Congregations 2015: Thriving and Surviving" documented some impervious factors related to growing churches. Fastest-growing churches were found in new suburbs where the population was growing. You cannot do anything about that if you are not located there. Large congregations with plentiful programs to meet the needs of all ages grew faster than small country churches. The study found that "small congregations face any number of uphill battles in terms of vitality and viability. Not all small congregations struggle, of course, but on average they do so more than larger congregations. Thus, the steady and dramatic increase in the number of congregations with under a hundred people in attendance for weekend worship must be pause for concern."[1] Yet you cannot do anything about that except to celebrate what you do well: worship God, serve others, reframe your goals to grow spiritually, and be glad for how you meet the needs of your people. Nevertheless, you can embrace certain ingredients for building attendance found in this book regardless of your location or size. Do what you can do and find the courage to change what can be changed.

First Attenders May Not Have the Same Interests as Long-Term Members

Not all first attenders and church shoppers are looking to the church for their sense of community, belonging, or activity. Some long-term members delight in creating a church to meet the emotional "belongingness" needs of members. These individuals use the word *community* so frequently that it makes you wonder if that is their real religion.

On the other hand, first attenders may be less interested in meeting their belongingness needs and more interested in seeking spiritual renewal. They are looking for a worship service that leads to an encounter with God, a church school that models values to their children, and an educational program to inform, inspire, and challenge their growth as people of faith. What happens? They arrive at church for ten minutes-worth of announcements about committee meetings, the church rummage sale, youth car wash, and church supper, and a report about how the church is not meeting its budget. That's not what they are seeking. For these guests, coffee hour is not necessarily a plus and may be beyond their comfort level. Passing the peace may be a time of teeth gritting with the hope that it will pass quickly.

To increase attendance, recognize that you must appeal to people with interests different from yours. View the worship service, especially the opening parts, through the lenses of first attenders. Immediately you view one of the greatest threats to growing your church: *change.*

Consider an old joke: "How many members of the congregation does it take to change a lightbulb?" Answer: "My grandmother gave that lightbulb to the church twenty-five years ago. Change? Change! We don't change."

How will you deal with this threat to growing your church? Suddenly two apparently different and possibly conflicting needs raise their heads: the need of longtimers who cherish feeling like a family of old friends, which is a blessed tie that binds them but which also has the potential to repel new people, whose primary need is an encounter with God. They aren't looking to crash a family gathering of longtime friends; they desire a worship experience that raises their spirits up to God.

Seeking only to meet the needs of potential new attenders could unravel the interweaving of old friendships and ties and cause a diminishing attendance when those needs are met less and less. On the other hand, seeking to preserve only the feelings of "belonging" and "family" may alienate or exclude first attenders who feel left out of the human interactions and who don't find the divine connection either.

Do you see the problem? If so, good, because naming the challenge is the necessary first step to finding ways to meet both needs. Is there a solution? The solution is to name the challenge and then bring together your best minds to work on it. Trust that smart people with good problem-solving skills will pool their ideas and resources to find a way. The group mind supersedes the individual mind when searching for institutional solutions.

Most First Attenders Do Not Care about Your History— At Least Not Now

The majority of church shoppers and first attenders are not interested in a church's history, yet what do congregations often highlight in their church logo, letterhead, bulletin cover, ads, and printed or electronic materials? Answer: how old the church is. Churches possess a lot of dignified history, and sometimes they relish showing it off in prime spaces. Generally speaking, that is not what church shoppers are attracted to, and it may even be a turnoff if your storied history appears frayed or worn. Searchers are looking for a place to have their spiritual needs met, not a historic organization whose emphasis on its age might suggest that the church is more interested in preserving and conserving its past than looking ahead to a bright, hopeful future.

First-time attenders are most often searching for a place that will meet their spiritual needs, that provides a worship service that leads them into an encounter with the Divine, that offers the possibility of belonging to a community of like-minded people, and that engages their mind, spirit, and hope. Is that what your letterhead proclaims? Or does it say, "Founded in 1811"? When visitors come into the entrance, do they view a glass-encased silver communion set from days gone by or a huge, two-hundred year-old Bible? Or do they feel they are entering a community of faithful people who long to connect today's contemporary challenges and issues with the teachings of Jesus? Look at modern advertising: advertisers are not promoting "old" but "new." Help first-time attenders become attracted to how your church connects to their current interests. Then later they may care about the history.

The Test of a Growth-Oriented Church Program

Do your church's newsletter and weekly bulletin feature programs that anyone with an interest could attend, or is it mostly about infrastructure?

Guests and members alike should be able to read the newsletter and determine that there are two or three programs of interest each month: adult education classes; affinity groups; musical concerts; opportunities to attend or participate in discussions connecting current events with spiritual faith; Bible studies; slide shows illustrating the travels of members; or after-worship programs for people who are already present. The key questions potential participants ask themselves are these: *What would I like to attend? What should I place on my schedule? What do I not want to miss, for the opportunity might not present itself again?*

To carry the test further, a strong and faithful church will promote a 2 to 1 ratio of programs for people to attend over information and data about boards, committees, meetings, and governance. This is an easy test to analyze: take your church's newsletter and tally which listings promote interesting possibilities for anyone to attend versus which are about infrastructure. If there is not a good handful of engaging possibilities that attract *you*, shift the balance away from *us* and toward *them*.

Suppose that, as a busy potential church attender, you would sacrifice anything in your schedule to connect to a like-minded group of people to meet once a week or once a month to discuss your mutual interests. What you do not want is the Wednesday night prayer group, which has been meeting together every week for half a century or a weekday Bible discussion that involves the same half dozen people who always attend. You want something new that speaks to *your* needs, interests, values, and beliefs. Then you open the newsletter online or on paper and see that the only thing listed on the calendar is committee meetings, the weekly prayer meeting, and an ongoing Bible study led by the pastor. You are grateful that the offerings meet the needs of some people, but you'll take a pass.

Now consider a different scenario. What if you saw listed a program or study that interested you? Perhaps it invited all newer attenders rather than just longtime members. Perhaps you would feel like *you* might be attracted to this new offering, along with others like you. Rather than feeling as if you were crashing a party of old, familiar friends, you could become a part of something new and interesting to you. Would you give it a try?

The test of a growth-oriented church is that its newsletter, bulletin, and listing of programs beckon anyone who might attend and benefit from the information rather than producing nothing more than infrastructure, board meetings, and in-house, long-term items that only regular insiders would find interesting. Wrestle with your church's newsletter. Design it to speak to all, including new attenders. Weigh its value by how it attracts the attention of everyone and not just insiders. Re-create it to offer at least two-thirds of its content to programs and opportunities for participation, other than reinforcing the current infrastructure of the institutional church.

Everybody Wants Young Adults

Congregations with many senior adults tend not to be growing while those with young adults tend to be growing. Congregations where one-third or more are seniors are less likely to grow than churches where one-third or less are seniors. Declining congregations have a much less promising track record in engaging young adults, which in turn is an obstacle to growth. The "American Congregations 2015" study discovered that young adult ministry is not really a priority in nearly half of American congregations and is the top priority of only one in ten. The study showed that congregations that make young adult ministry their top priority are about five times more likely to have a thriving young adult ministry than congregations for which it is not a priority.

The reality is that young adults are less interested and participate less in organized religion, although many still define themselves as "spiritual but not religious," which gives some indication that they hold spiritual needs. Further, it may not be possible for small congregations to invest heavily to make a young adult ministry a top priority. And yet research shows that such a priority yields growth. Perhaps the best strategy for most small churches is to do whatever you can do to be attractive to young adults, cherish the ones you already have, and bump up this priority a notch or two to attempt to do a little more to meet the spiritual needs of this generation. Consider gathering some of your young adults into a focus group (see chapter 10) to discover how to best meet their needs and to determine which programs might best increase their attendance and participation. See Denise Janssen's book *Reclaimed: Faith in an Emerging Generation* (Judson Press, 2015) for ideas that keep young adults connected to the church.

Research, Research, Research

Inform your decisions by questioning what works, what is worth the investment, and why you should bother with this ingredient for the sake of growing the church. Ask people questions. Ask your leaders to ask people questions. Use surveys and rating scales to provide data. Why did they come: Worship? Christian education? Music? Biblical preaching? A quiet hour?

One congregation invested heavily in a teen youth program. Members loved seeing teenagers reading Scripture, ushering, washing cars, and going on mission trips. But when they researched to ask new members what drew them to the church, it was not the youth program but the Christian education and music programs—both of which were funded at considerably less than the investment in youth. That does not suggest cutting a popular program, but it may inform that new funds would be well invested in the primary reasons that draw new attenders to the church.

Another church underwrote a musical concert series for the public, believing that all the attention and advertising would draw potential new attenders to worship. The series was worth doing for its own merits, but when they researched, they found that over a three-year period not one visitor attended worship as a result of the concert series. Another church, after asking church shoppers why they selected their church, discovered that the primary draw was the warmth of the welcome. As a consequence, they invested talent, resources, and staffing to build on that strength, increasing even more the appeal to new church shoppers.

As you build your strategic plan to meet the spiritual needs of more people in your community, ask and ask and ask. Use data to inform your decision-making about where to invest money, time, and talent to build attendance. Part 3 includes sections about surveys and focus groups. Also attempt to evaluate results numerically. Create the habit of volunteers and leaders being asked if their program or idea has brought in new attenders or increased attendance over the past year.

Most churches do not need sophisticated research models because they are small enough to base their research results on anecdotal evidence. If, for example, your church decided to institute an annual play with many participants from the congregation, that alone may have benefit for entertainment, fellowship, and a fun activity. It is also worth asking the play's leaders, "Based on your observations, how has the play brought in new people to the worship life of our community on a regular basis? Can you name some of the people who are now regular attenders or members because the play brought them in?" Assure these leaders that perhaps the play's purpose may not be to attract new people or build attendance, and that is fine. But if it is designed for growing the church, cite anecdotal observations of how it worked.

Invest Where It Does the Most Good

Your goal is to build attendance and attract new members to your congregation where their spiritual needs can be met. Analyze carefully what investments over the years have yielded results. You do not want to offend anyone, but there are always some who believe incorrectly that their program might possibly attract new members. For example, concerts available to the community rarely yield much by way of increased worship attendance. They have significant other value but are not a vehicle for growing the church. Weddings for nonmembers may be a source of revenue and offer a service to the community, but they are rarely an opportunity to gain new interest in the faith community. In this digital age, newspaper ads are generally a waste of money and exist primarily to placate a minority of existing members who like to see their church listed in the paper.

Your church possesses precious few resources to invest. Choose wisely where the returns are likely to increase attendance and to meet the spiritual needs of more new people. It is better to invest in a few things well than to spread your resources too thin.

NOTES

1. David A. Roozen, "American Congregations 2015: Thriving and Surviving," Hartford Institute for Religion Research, accessed January 12, 2018, http://hirr.hartsem.edu/American-Congregations-2015.pdf, 2.

Chapter 3
Setting Goals

Declare That You Want to Meet More Needs

How can you inspire your church to be intentional about increasing attendance? Declare at every board and committee meeting that you want to meet more needs. Make it an agenda item: "What can our group do to grow attendance?" Involve the entire congregation in the conversation. Consider an all-member retreat or a specially called church meeting to discuss your desire to meet more needs. Frame increasing attendance theologically. Set the stage for the conversations by discussing the right reasons to desire increase in attendance: to meet the spiritual needs of more people. Then keep the focus on meeting needs.

When conversation turns to the church's needs (for example, to fill seats, get more money, increase the pool of volunteers), use that conversation as a teaching moment to reframe thinking. Nothing is wrong with a church wanting to grow to sustain its vitality, but how much more exciting it is to want to grow for the sake of meeting the needs of more people in your area. Begin by declaring that this is what you desire to do. Intentionality is a proven necessity to increasing attendance. Perhaps it is the most important ingredient, for if a congregation is clear about its goals and is willing to invest energy and resources to achieve those goals, it is far more likely to hit the target at which it aims.

Set Some Specific Measurable Objectives for the Year

The *disadvantage* of setting specific measureable objectives is that meeting the objectives may supersede the theological imperative to meet the spiritual needs of more people in the community. The *advantage* is that the goal remains ever in the minds of leadership and staff. Many people are goal-oriented. If given a goal and the freedom to discover ways to achieve the goal, they will burst with creativity and initiatives to accomplish the goal. For example, one goal may be to build the choir(s) to a ratio of one choir member per ten attenders. By the end of the year, it is simple to tally the numbers to determine if the goal has been accomplished or not.

If the Christian education staff, teachers, and committee members embrace the increased attendance goal as a high priority, they can do a lot to contribute to the goal. When children are motivated to want to come to church school, there is a good chance their parents will attend too—children do not drive, so parents must bring them. One inexpensive and easy strategy for building attendance is to purchase preprinted postcards from a church supply house to send to children, letting them know they are missed and that their teacher is looking forward to seeing them again soon. Adding a brief handwritten note increases the impact.

The leader of a youth group was complimented on the continued growth in numbers and attendance. "You must be doing something right," said the one paying the compliment. The youth leader replied, "It doesn't happen by itself. I get on the phone and send texts and emails starting midweek and constantly check in with the youth to invite them and tell them I'd enjoy having them join me on Sunday."

The challenge is not so much discovering good ideas to build attendance but building and sustaining the ownership and enthusiasm of the staff and volunteers to *want* to build attendance. If in the planning stage the staff and volunteers play a major role in adopting the goal and setting for themselves a few measurable objectives, they are much more likely to hit the target because they are aiming at it.

Emphasize Attendance, Not Membership

Emphasizing attendance rather than membership may feel counter-intuitive. When pastors talk about their churches, one of the first pieces of data they share is their church's size by number of members. When denominations request funding from their churches, they often assess by the number of members (although they frown upon the term *head tax*). One may glean from this that when it comes to status or finance, membership is the currency. But for theological purposes of setting out to meet the needs of more people, attendance is the value. Count the number of people in the pews, not the number of names on the rolls. That is an easy measure to substantiate and a gauge to tell if attendance is growing, declining, or holding its own. It is also plainly visible to worship participants. Most are likely to possess only a vague idea of how many members the church has, but they can see for themselves whether the seats are full or empty.

What's more, there is a major shift in our culture today toward attending or participating rather than joining, belonging, or becoming members. If a church talks in language of membership, it could alienate those who are not interested in official membership. In contrast, if you use language of participation and attendance, you address the thinking of everyone who walks through the sanctuary door.

Emphasizing participation can also include those who engage in the church's programs and ministries, even if they are not attending Sunday morning worship. When considering participation, would you not include those in the nursery, church school, hospitality, or other programs? They are present in service to God and their church even if they are not sitting in a pew that week. Of course their participation counts toward attendance. But wait: why not also count those who participate in church softball teams, host concerts, and work at or attend church fairs and suppers? Then you can report that 150 people participated in worship or Sunday morning programs and *also* that 50 people participated in weekday or weekend programs and ministries. They count too and ought to be included in the emphasis on participation more than membership.

Swimming against the Tide May Get You Nowhere

Especially at the beginning when early successes boost enthusiasm and hope, avoid choosing goals that swim against the tide. For example, suppose when you observe the makeup of your current congregation, you see that they are older and graying. In particular, suppose you notice a lack of twentysomethings in your congregation. It is natural for every congregation to want to rebalance their age range to tilt a few decades younger by setting out to attract more young adults. "They are the future of the church," proclaim the stalwarts.

Consider a couple of realities. First, a large percent of twentysomethings in the United States have never set foot inside of a church building. Second, the fastest-growing age demographic in church attendance is age sixty-five and older. Every church seems to want the twentysomethings, and nobody seems inclined to attract the golden agers. Reality check: What makes you think you can do what nobody else is doing, to attract the twentysomethings? Pour energy and resources into this goal and next year you will be making excuses for why it failed.

On the other hand, the readiness and receptivity of the AARP (American Association of Retired Persons) set is highly responsive to any small initiative you might extend. So do not fight the tide. Invest where your investment does the most good, produces the most fruit, and is appreciated. If your seats become filled with a grayer congregation, so what? At least it is becoming filled rather than emptied. Start with those who are most likely to want to come. Then involve those in their twenties and thirties to design goals to attract their peers and meet the needs of those age cohorts.

Avoid the Sisyphus Syndrome

In Greek mythology, Sisyphus was a king of Ephyra (now known as Corinth). He was punished for chronic deceitfulness by being compelled to roll an immense boulder up a hill, only to watch it roll back down, repeating this action forever. Your attempts to build attendance may feel like pushing an immense boulder up a hill, only to watch it roll back down again.

We live in a time of declining church membership and attendance. That is the culture that surrounds people of faith. Add to
that the possibility that your church may be in a declining demographic where citizens are vacating your zip code. Stir in to your
mix every ingredient in this book and you may still find that your
attendance declines or barely holds the line. If the culture and the
population dynamics diminish your best attempts, stop rolling the
boulder up the hill and do not beat yourself up for lack of results.
When attempts do not yield results, do not repeat doing more of
the same. If you are sincerely trying your best to meet the spiritual needs of people and nothing is working, focus instead on your
strengths. Celebrate what you do have, what you can do, and how
God is using your church to meet the spiritual needs of those who
come. Never do less than your best for the ones who need you most.

Chapter 4
Ongoing Management

Keep the Message Ever before the Congregation:
"Our Church Meets Needs"

Keeping the message "Our church meets needs" ever before your congregation is vital. Never let the flame of that candle go out. Over time, as members hear again and again about how their church meets the spiritual needs of people, they will internalize the message and be more inclined to spread the word to others. They will be proud that "Our church meets needs well and there are more people in our area with needs that we could meet."

Nothing is more effective in convincing members that their church meets needs than the testimony of its own members in telling their own stories. When they speak from the pulpit, share during a time of prayer concerns, publish good news in the newsletter, or witness from the website, the message is reinforced: "This church meets my needs." Celebrate it, tell about it, record it, remember it, and encourage more and more stories to fortify the message that your church meets spiritual needs more uniquely than any other human organization. Those who might consider attending are not attracted because your church is old, historic, busy, or needy. They will be attracted because of the hope that you might be able to meet their needs. *People do not attend because a church is needy. They attend because a church meets needs.*

Celebrate Success

Avoid the Eeyore effect. Eeyore is an old, gray, stuffed donkey in the Winnie-the-Pooh books by A. A. Milne. Eeyore is characterized by his pessimistic, gloomy, depressed, and negative outlook. If there is a beautiful, sunny, blue sky with only one small, gray cloud, Eeyore will point out the imperfection. Oh, how church leaders can do the same.

An affluent congregation enjoyed the pleasure of one budget surplus after another, only to announce at the next annual meeting that, essentially, *You should worry because next year will be worse.* At the conclusion of that predicted worse year, another surplus was reached, but the Eeyore leaders continued to squelch celebrations of success with dire predictions that the worst is yet to come. They decreased morale, raised a feeling of alarm, inspired zero change in giving, and underbudgeted so that the staff and program suffered no increase year after year. The end-of-year surplus went to the building reserves and contingency fund, not to the staff or programs that began the year with cuts because of the warnings of alarm.

Why don't churches appreciate and celebrate success? Successful fund-raisers know that nobody wants to support a sinking ship. Rather, givers want to support the hope of meeting more needs. So when your church has a success in growing attendance, celebrate it. Tell about it in worship, in the newsletter, in the annual report, at the annual meeting, and in meetings of the governing board. Celebrate! Enjoy. Allow yourselves the luxury of feeling good about your achievement. To celebrate does not diminish new efforts. Lifting up success inspires. Negating accomplishments deflates and lowers morale. If you can point to an increase in attendance, name it, detail it, thank those involved, and celebrate that you have met more needs.

Form an Attendance Development Group

Convene an attendance development group to work on the goal of growing your church, perhaps over a year's time. Key question: "How can we meet the spiritual needs of more people in our community? If we estimate that we could meet the needs of a hundred more people in the next five years, what would it take to achieve that goal?" Handpick participants for this group. Rather than selecting the usual church leaders, select individuals who are CEOs, business executives, nonprofit directors, and leaders in marketing, sales, and advertising—people with experience and wisdom about building up a business or clientele.

The key here is transferability: What can transfer from this group's goal-oriented successes to the church? Obviously not everything transfers, but why not begin with people who know the most about reaching and attracting others? Consider making this group's function different from that of other church committees, perhaps meeting monthly with the pastor at a private home over dinner. You might ask a staff member to be present to take notes. Clearly identify the goal and stay fixed on it: to build attendance over the long run.

In addition to strategic plans that might emerge, the swirl of activity created by this group may by itself result in heightened attention to building attendance. It is also possible that some of the members may have the capability and motivation to underwrite some of the attendance building projects. Do not underestimate the possibility of private contributions to fund experiments and new ventures. Note this word of caution: secure the blessing of your church's governing board in advance to engender their sense of ownership. Otherwise they may not embrace the group's recommendations later.

As you begin to meet with your attendance development group, explain why they were handpicked to advise the pastor and senior leaders of the congregation—because of their experience, know-how, and savvy. Encourage them to apply to the church what they have learned from their marketing and promotion experiences. These people are goal achievers. Together dream up some goals of what could be possible. Then watch with fascination how they recommend and provide leadership to pursuing those goals. George Bernard Shaw said, "Some people see things as they are and ask 'why?' Others dream things that could be and ask 'why not?'"

Allow these dreamers and doers to apply the best of their skills to growing the church and building attendance.

Link Attendance Growth to Staff Job Descriptions and Performance Evaluations

If the congregation has named growing the church and building attendance as a priority for their staff, affirm that priority by listing it as a job description expectation. Then when the staff members are evaluated for their annual performance review, let them know they will be accountable for how they have contributed to this goal. This is putting the proverbial money where the mouth is.

Staff report to a supervisor, although in some congregations this is an ambiguous mixture of volunteer leaders and senior staff. Make it clear to whoever does the evaluating of staff that attendance growth is a named congregational priority and an expectation. If staff are not comfortable with this goal, help them to educate themselves to retool or to begin their search for employment that better meets their personal comfort level and needs. Nothing drives effort toward achieving a goal better than clearly stated expectations about how a paid staff member will be evaluated.

If the congregation has not clearly identified growing the church and building attendance as an institutional priority, be cautious. Listing it in job descriptions or holding staff accountable for making it happen can backfire on you by causing division and conflict. And so the necessary prerequisite to using the staff to implement the church's priorities is for the church to state clearly, by congregational vote if appropriate, what the church's institutional priorities are.

Be careful here, for if existing staff were hired under previous job descriptions and then the church votes to modify priorities, the staff must also own the new priority or else renegotiate the terms of their employment. But new staff can be employed with new job descriptions and accountability. "You were hired to coordinate the music program" can become "You are hired to coordinate the music program and grow the number of people who participate in it." Or, "You were hired to direct the educational program" adds growing the number of participants and attenders. And the new pastor's job description (and annual evaluation) is reconstructed to free the pastor to attend to growing the church and building attendance, recognizing that some of the traditional responsibilities must be moved to the "do not do" list or be assigned to others to liberate the pastor to attend to the church's stated priorities.

Annual performance reviews for all staff members consider not only the accomplishments, strengths, and lists of work completed but also how that staff member has endeavored to grow attendance and participation.

Establish a System to Prevent Attenders from Falling through the Cracks

Establish a protocol for regularly asking, "Who has not been here for a while?" Discussion of this question may be an agenda item for every meeting of the deacons, elders, or pastoral staff. By asking this question, you establish an ongoing safety net so that people do not fall through the cracks. Do not put this key question on the end of the agenda when everyone is tired and yearning to go home. Give it prime time and prime importance. Ask deacons to name names of those who they have not seen for a few Sundays. Design a strategy for who should contact them: a phone call is better than an email, especially if it is made by the right person who knows them.

Flush out reasons for the missing persons' lack of attendance. Are they unhappy about something? Better to know than not to know. Do they have health or financial problems that make them hesitant to attend? Or, is it that they have children in youth sports that meet on Sundays and they will return when the sports season concludes? Taking time to determine who is missing and then giving them a call is one of the most effective safety nets for catching worship participants who have fallen away and has a successful record of reengaging them. If well managed, this agenda item need not take long, so make it a prime agenda item each month and reinforce to the deacons and other pastoral caregivers their own commitment to building attendance and reducing attrition.

Hold Frequent New Member Classes

Each church establishes its own practices for how to prepare new people to become members, but notice that churches that raise the bar too high and require too many classes generally have the best-designed program with the least results. Consider: most people who want to join your church have already been attending for a while and know what they are getting into.

Holding new member classes quarterly or more frequently is preferable so that each new member class is smaller and more intimate. Even if no one shows up, you establish a routine pattern that signals the congregation that building membership remains a goal. Make becoming a member easily accessible. Provide free child care if you are hoping to attract young families. Light refreshments also serve as an ice breaker as people wait for the class to begin.

Emphasize attendance more than membership, but make membership easily available. Do not overwhelm potential new members with data about your governance, history, and denomination. Invite a few (but not too many) church leaders or staff to join you to provide information to those exploring membership. Emphasize that the class is to explore and there is no obligation for them to join if they would prefer to wait. Balance the time carefully between providing information and allowing those exploring membership to tell about themselves and interact with one another.

Continue to Orient New Members after They Have Joined

Some churches are moving toward reducing the number of classes required for new members to join and increasing the number of follow-up opportunities for new members to gather, sometimes over brunch or a meal, to continue learning about their church and their denomination. A couple of times a year, have the deacons or the new members committee hold a meal for all those who have joined the church within the past two years. Bring in church leaders to talk about their areas of responsibility, educational leaders to tell about new opportunities, and new member mentors to come alongside those who desire mentoring. Also invite as guests the families of those who have joined.

Such an opportunity reinforces attendance, reduces attrition (more on this below), increases members' knowledge about their congregation, and builds bonds among the newest members. From that time on, the new members will have an ongoing relationship with others who joined with them in that class. Continuing to orient new members after they have joined frees the church from having to cram everything into one or two new member classes prior to joining.

Remind Members to Invite Others

You might think that members would invite others without being reminded, but it never hurts to repeat the message. Suggest that members use the telephone rather than email to contact someone, or to invite a friend or neighbor they happen to encounter. Make it easy for your people to invite others by suggesting words they might use. Perhaps they might link the personal invitation to a special Sunday feature: "Sue, this Sunday our church is holding a blessing of the backpacks. I wondered if that might appeal to you and your children."

One leader who started a Thursday men's luncheon recruited a sidekick to assist him with coordinating the program. At first there were six to eight men. That soon doubled to about fifteen, then doubled again and again until there were about eighty men attending every Thursday luncheon. His sidekick remarked on how the lunch was drawing the attention of so many. The leader explained why: "I get on the phone starting on Monday and every day call men to ask if they will come to lunch on Thursday." Therein lies the key to building attendance. It does not happen by itself. Meeting the spiritual needs of more people takes planning, initiative, investment, coordination, and follow-up.

Watch the Back Door

There is not much point bringing new people in the front door if others are pouring out the back door. Prevent attrition. Especially for those without a lifetime's experience of attending church, they might take a Sunday off, skip another, and then figure it did not seem to hurt to miss two and so begin a pattern of dropping off in attending worship. The sooner you can reverse a pattern of dropping off, the more likely you will reinvigorate their enthusiasm and participation. Design safety nets to monitor and reduce attrition.

While you never want to give a sense that you are taking attendance, it is beneficial to let people know they are missed. Start with simple, brief, and easy outreach, perhaps an email from a deacon saying, "I've missed seeing you at church recently and wanted to check in to see if everything is okay." A one-line email or text like that lets an individual know that at least one person noticed she or he has not been present. After an absence of a couple of months, perhaps a phone call is more in order. If the deacon receives any indication that there might be a problem, the pastor can be notified to make contact.

Manage Your Money and How You Talk about It

The "American Congregations 2015" study found financial stress "is bad enough in and of itself, but it frequently becomes a major catalyst for a spiraling mix of other negative effects."[1] What effects? Increased levels of conflict. A direct connection exists between congregations with high financial stress and those with high conflict, both of which are detrimental to growing your church. High financial stress also contributed to a less positive sense of worship.

Not many options are available for dealing with church finances: either increase income or decrease expenses. Robbing the endowment to cover current expenses is to cannibalize yourself. Taking it out on your staff by not providing annual compensation increases can ultimately result in reduced morale or increased turnover. Recognize that financial stress sends ripples out to the pews, classrooms, choir loft, committee meetings, and every other aspect of a congregation's life.

What to do? First, craft a healthy long-term annual giving program that uses the best strategies to build an emphasis on growing the generosity of members year after year. See *Beyond Stewardship: A Church Guide to Generous Giving* by John Zehring and Kate

Jagger (Judson Press, 2016) for guidance on how to create and sustain an annual giving campaign that is giver-centered.

Second, reframe how you talk about your money. When you achieve a goal or succeed in meeting a budget, celebrate, celebrate, and celebrate. Do not meet success with "Just wait, next year will be worse." Talk about the abundance that God has blessed you with. Eliminate words and attitudes about scarcity. Be transparent and honest about the church's finances, but temper your communication by lifting up what you have done and can do to meet needs with the resources you have.

Third, create a written investment advisory policy to guide the management of your endowed resources. You need not reinvent the wheel. Ask your denomination for names of churches that already have such policies, and get copies of those policies. Generations of churches have created healthy written policies just as generations have been poor stewards because they lacked or did not follow wise investment guidelines. The way churches manage and talk about money is a reflection of their faith and their theology. Use language of abundance rather than scarcity. Then encourage members to hold the faith to go and do likewise.

See through Lenses of Abundance Rather Than Lenses of Scarcity

Many congregations perseverate about what they do not have or what they cannot do. They whine about not having enough money, enough members, or enough teachers, and about a facility that is not good enough. That is seeing through lenses of scarcity. You choose which lenses you see through, so choose to see the abundance in your midst. Name it. Promote it. Tell about what you do have and can do. Celebrate what is good about your church.

Inform members that seeing through lenses of abundance will be your mind-set. You are neither naïve nor unrealistic, but you understand that the words you choose determine your attitude, and the attitude you adopt determines your behavior and your feelings about yourself. Therefore, reframe how your congregation talks about and thinks about itself. Hold constantly before your people the abundance God has blessed you with. Put the way you describe your mission, ministry, service, and work into the positive. God does not call your church to be successful. God does not call your church to be busy. God does not call your church to be popular. What God calls your church to be is *faithful*. Emphasize faithfulness. Efforts to meet the needs of more people is a by-product of your faithfulness, but if the culture and demographics prevent results, shift gears to work on growing in faithfulness to God. See through lenses of abundance and meet the spiritual needs of those who are already coming.

NOTES

1. David A. Roozen, "American Congregations 2015: Thriving and Surviving," Hartford Institute for Religion Research, accessed January 12, 2018, http://hirr.hartsem.edu/American-Congregations-2015.pdf, 7.

Chapter 5

Low-Cost Investments
Some Gain Potential

When it comes to making changes for attendance growth in your church, begin by plucking the low-hanging fruit. You do not have to do everything all at once. Identify goals that have a high payoff with a minimum of energy or investment. Begin with easy goals that might lead to visible results. The impact of generating a number of short-term wins encourages leaders and members that building attendance is achievable. Don't forget to celebrate every small success by telling about it.

In planning sessions it can be helpful to brainstorm many possibilities and then put a star next to the low-hanging fruit that can be accomplished sooner rather than later. Do not overwhelm church leaders by too long a list of things that could be done. (That being said, planners may also want to place a mark next to items that might be stage two or stage three goals to attempt.) Choose to do a few things well rather than trying to accomplish too much at once.

Provide a Cordial Welcome and Introductory Instructions

A personal welcome and introductory instructions set the stage before a new attender enters the sanctuary. Personal greeters should be stationed at entrances for the half hour before the service begins. Most congregations do that. But are your greeters trained? To do what? How will they recognize a first-time attender? What should greeters say to them? Will being greeted in a particular way make a guest's entrance more or less comfortable? Do greeters subsequently hand off first-time attenders to ushers who will escort them to their seats? Greeters and ushers should put first-time attenders at ease about where to sit. (Have you ever entered an unfamiliar worship place for the first time, and feared that you might be sitting in some longtime member's "regular" pew?)

A welcome table at the sanctuary entrance (not off in a far corner) can provide a handsome packet of introductory information about the church and its ministries. The care by which a church informs new attenders through simple literature will broadcast a message far beyond the pages about how it cares—or doesn't care—that they have come to be with you this morning. So be sure not to overwhelm. This is not the place to include every brochure the church ever produced. Consider which information visitors would benefit from as a brief orientation. Include a basic brochure about the church, the educational program, a map of the facility, and perhaps a short description of what will happen in the worship service, including whether there will be an opportunity for visitors to be recognized or introduce themselves.

Out-of-date or worn-looking materials do more harm than good. It communicates that your church does not care enough to keep its information up-to-date. If your materials feature staff who are no longer at the church, past activities from the previous year, or programs that no longer exist, that is an embarrassment to the church. If the brochures are not current and attractive, dump them in the recycle bin.

New attenders are used to up-to-the-second information everywhere else in their lives. Consider producing a simple, attractive, and easy-to-update brochure for first-time attenders. Write it in plain language without religious jargon, keeping in mind people who have no church background. Tell guests what to expect, what the worship service is designed to do, where to park, where to hang their coats, whether or not they should wear name tags, and any special practices of the church. (May or should they take communion? How do they know when to stand or kneel? What happens during the passing of the peace?)

Be sure to describe what happens after the worship service as well. Is the postlude a time for gathering personal belongings and beginning personal chitchat or a time of reverent silence that puts a seal on the worship experience? How can they meet the pastor or other church leaders? Are they invited to join the congregation for coffee hour—and if so, where is it?

Your greeters and ushers should also be intentional about reconnecting with visitors to extend a personal invitation and escort to your fellowship hour as desired. Such time for informal conversation may be cherished by longtime members, but it can be a daunting experience for first-time attenders. An invitation for them to join you is lovely, but not if they are left to stand around and hope someone will come up and talk to them. Appoint some of your most hospitable and gregarious members to serve as hosts during coffee hour, connecting with first-time attenders and staying close to handle introductions to the pastor or deacons, to the minister of music and children's ministry leaders, and to other church members as well.

Good Signage Signals Guests That They Are a Priority

Longtime members do not need directions to the restrooms. Many may think it is obvious where the sanctuary, the fellowship hall, or the highly used meeting rooms are located. First-time visitors, on the other hand, may stand at the entrance scratching their heads and wondering whether to go up or down, right or left, to the sanctuary. Every entrance should have signs pointing to the sanctuary. Every entrance should have signs for the restrooms, including unisex and handicap accessible options. Would someone searching for the church office know how to get there from the entrance—or which entrance to use for the office? Would first-time visitors know where to take their children for church school? Pair directional signs with nearby information racks.

For example, imagine that a young family with children enters the church for the first time on a Sunday morning and immediately sees a sign that (a) says where children go at the beginning, often in worship, (b) indicates where the classrooms are located (in case parents want to view in advance), (c) offers photos of the teachers or leaders by age group, and (d) provides a brochure telling about the church's educational program for children. What do you think that a young family with children is thinking? Answer: *Here is a church that wants us and caters to our needs.*

On the flip side: a young family with children enters, and untrained greeters handing out bulletins do not recognize them as visitors. If the young family sees no signage or information about the programs for their children, what do you imagine those parents are thinking? Answer: *Here is a church that does not seem to be equipped to welcome young families. Maybe we've come to the wrong place.* What a crazy irony that every church drools at the thought of attracting more young families, and yet the first impression they make is that they really do not care.

Good signage communicates far more than basic directions; good signage proclaims that a church cares about its guests. Further, good signs may help to remind regular members to view entering and getting around their facility through the eyes of guests.

Improve Parking Information

Parking is a conundrum. As consumers, people expect parking to be ample and in proximity to the front door, as exemplified by big-box stores and major groceries. Large suburban churches may be able to imitate that example, including plentiful handicap-permit parking spaces and excellent lighting for evening services and other ministry programs. However, many churches were built when worshippers arrived by horse or trolley. Their parking lots are small or nonexistent. Some urban churches can offer only on-street parking. A few churches have experimented with valet parking, particularly for older or handicapped members, but valet parking is difficult to sustain over a long period, and there are liability issues to consider. What to do?

If you cannot improve your parking, what you can improve is your information about where to park. Members already know where to park. Those who attend only Christmas and Easter services may expect to park a distance away on those days. But what about people who are investigating the idea of attending your church? Those are the ones whose spiritual needs you are attempting to meet. Your website is the number one place most church shoppers will turn to find out about you, so either make the website oriented to those exploring or at least have a special tab easily selected just for them. Look at the website through the eyes of someone who has never been to church and anticipate their needs and how to put their concerns at ease. Recognize that their first questions are "How do I enter?" and "Where do I park?" Use maps and descriptions of where and how to park, including where the entrance of the parking lot is or where passengers may be dropped off at the most accessible entrance. If possible, list a GPS address for the entrance to the parking area. If on-street parking has meters, state clearly whether it is free on Sundays or if they must pay. Use photos showing where people park on the street, and add pictures of people entering the church being greeted and shown to the welcome table.

Attend to Those Guests Who Fall into Your Lap

When people first visit your church, how do you greet them? How do you follow up their visit? Isn't it amazing how congregations can devote extraordinary attention to trying to attract new people, only to neglect them when they show up on the church's doorstep? Are they welcomed personally by a greeter? Is there a deacon, church leader, or staff member whose job it is to watch for first attenders and introduce them to the pastor and offer to escort them to coffee hour? Are they offered a packet of information or at least an up-to-date brochure? If they have children, is a church leader present to explain what is available for children and introduce them personally to the church's education director, and perhaps even walk them to the classrooms so they can see where their children will go?

After their visit, how will you let them know that "we noticed you were with us"? Will they receive a phone call from a leader within twenty-four hours? Will the pastor send them a note card thanking them for their visit and extending a welcome to return?

What is your plan to ensure that they provide information about themselves, such as signing a guest book or visitor pew card? If visitors tell you they are "church shopping," that is a loud and clear indication that they have a need that you might be able to meet. They have reached out to you. If your goal is to build attendance, there is nothing more important you have to do than to be responsive to them. Design a plan for how you can give heightened attention to those who fall into your lap.

Offer to Visit If a Visit Is Desired

If guests *tell* you they are looking for a new church home, offer to visit them. Not all visitors will tell you this, but if they share that they are church shopping, that may be a signal that they would welcome a personal visit from a staff member or senior leader. What if the other churches they shop visit them and you do not? What if you visit and the others do not? It has been said, "Eighty percent of the job is just showing up." Showing up demonstrates that you care enough to reach out. Personal visits with "church shoppers" can be time-consuming; a church can sustain the practice long-term only when building attendance is a stated and supported goal of the church.

One couple in their seventies were church shopping. The next week, the pastor visited them. They told the pastor, "This is the first time in our lives that we have had the pleasure of having a pastor in our home." For the pastor, it is probably one of many visits that week, hundreds in a year. For the person being visited, it may be a once-in-a-lifetime experience. It will be remembered, cherished, and valued.

For that reason, those who tell you that they are looking for a church home should go to the top of the pastor's visit list, right after tragedies and emergencies. The potential gain is high, especially if the visit occurs shortly after they attend worship. In surveys that study why new attenders return and remain at churches, the pastor is the second-highest reason (the first is being personally invited or accompanied by a member). If there are too many church shoppers for the pastor to visit (wouldn't that be a nice problem?), use other staff and senior leaders to make the personal connections. Does the individual or couple have young children or teenagers? Ask the Christian education director or youth leader to visit. Use a senior leader of the church (moderator or president) and the chairs of boards for visits. But no matter what, show up. Eighty percent of the job is just showing up.

Identify People Ready to Find a Home Church

Identify people with a heightened readiness to find a church. These individuals will be most open to receiving invitations to visit your congregation and get involved. Brainstorm with your deacons, care team, congregational leaders, and church staff to list categories of people who might be most receptive to a church that desires to meet their spiritual needs. For example, people who are recently divorced may welcome a personal invitation along with the company of a member to attend worship with them.

Similarly, those who have lost a spouse or other loved one often experience a heightened interest in connecting with a community of faith. One woman described how, after her husband had died, her neighbor Peggy invited her to come to church with her. "I was lonely and ready to find a church community," explained the new widow. Peggy was wise to recognize someone who might be seeking a church and quick to make a personal invitation. Later the women became good friends at the church, usually sitting side-by-side in worship, chatting at coffee hour, and participating in adult education programs together.

Many people testify about how one person made the difference by inviting them to come at just the right time in their lives. Be mindful that walking into a new church for the first time can be a daunting experience for anyone, but for a person who has been part of a couple for years (or decades!), she or he may find it especially awkward or uncomfortable to be suddenly single. Sitting alone in a pew may be sufficient reason not to attend for some. Entering the fellowship hall for coffee hour alone could be terrifying. Recently divorced persons may also wonder if they will be judged by others for the dissolution of their marriage.

Encourage your members to reach out to bereaved or divorced neighbors or coworkers, and to make their invitation to visit your church a warm and personal one—and to go a step further by offering to drive the first-time attender or to at least arrange to meet the person in a specific location and sit with him or her during the service. A personal invitation that comes with assurance that the guest will be met by a familiar face, someone who will sit alongside during service and provide an escort and introductions during coffee hour, may determine whether that invitation is accepted.

Hold conversations among the deacons or care team about your congregation's ministry to those who have lost a spouse or partner. Put yourselves in their shoes. Enter the church as though for the first time and see it through their eyes. What can you change or add to provide a warm welcome to meet their needs? If the single-again visitor is seeking fellowship and renewed community, what ministries and programs offer the opportunity to meet other members and to form meaningful friendships? Coming alongside people facing a new need can be a vitally important way for a congregation to help them become a part of the family of faith.

What other categories of people might have a heightened readiness to attend church? People who are new to the neighborhood or have recently returned to the community? Inactive members who have faced a recent change or a challenge to their health, employment, or family status? Many people in our social circles will at sometime in their lives receive an unfavorable health diagnosis. "Would you consider coming to church with me?" could be a golden invitation at a time when their receptivity is high. Today even the highest-level professionals lose jobs because their employer downsized, reorganized, moved away, or eliminated the position. This can come as a shock to a worker who thought all was going well. Perhaps they have a readiness to add a spiritual dimension to how they process what is happening to them. What can it hurt to invite them to join you at church?

Being sensitive to those with a heightened readiness will yield a better response to your invitations than just randomly inviting people. Also remember, part of the effort to build attendance is to reactivate less-active members in addition to attracting new attenders. If you are acquainted with a member who has become inactive, you may sense that he or she may feel awkward about returning. The inactive member may want to return but does not want to be bombarded with well-meaning curiosity or misplaced humor. (Remember the long-absent family who was greeted with the comment, "Look who's coming to church today! Oh my, the walls of the church may come tumbling down.") Here is where more than a passing invitation could be cherished: "I'd love for you to see how things are going at the church. Would you come with me on Sunday? I will be happy to pick you up. Then perhaps we can go out to lunch afterward."

There are many other categories of people with a heightened readiness to find a new faith community or to return to the church they once attended. Identify those individuals or types of people and reach out to them.

Create Special Sundays

Add features to the worship service that bring people out to recognize or to celebrate. A New England church that experienced the usual decline in summer attendance created a late fall "Blessing of the Snowbirds" service to celebrate members who had gone south for the winter and had newly returned home for the warmer months. For that Sunday attendance was high.

Another congregation celebrated their tradition that "once a deacon, always a deacon," even after the term of active service concludes. They planned a Sunday when the "Permanent Diaconate" would be recognized, followed by a potluck lunch to honor them. Every member and former member of that congregation who had ever served as a deacon (at that church or any other) was mailed a special invitation, and during the service all came forward for a blessing. On that Sunday the building was packed.

For Pentecost another church planned in advance for everyone to wear something red. That Sunday red helium balloons accented every entrance, and red streamers and banners adorned the sanctuary. A jazz band was the musical centerpiece and played "When the

Saints Go Marching In" as the choir, children, and church school teachers processed in and then round and round the pews, surrounding the congregation in song. The service was a true celebration of the coming of the Holy Spirit, and on that Sunday attendance skyrocketed.

Do you see the pattern? Plan and create special Sundays when people will want to come and many will bring members of their extended family and their friends. Allow your creativity to think up what else could be a special Sunday: celebrations or recognitions of people in certain professions like education or health care, children's Sunday, youth Sunday, holy days in the Christian year and holidays in the Hallmark year, World Hunger Sunday, World Peace Sunday, and World Communion Sunday.

Select different boards or committees to be recognized and thanked within the worship service (have these members *ever* been thanked?), where their roles can be explained. For example, devote a section of the service for "recognition of our trustees," asking each to come forward, and at the end applauding the entire board for their faithful service. It is likely that attendance among trustees that Sunday will be high and include their families. Do the same for each board or committee. Hold a homecoming service in September to kick off the year, an anniversary service to recognize people who have been members for twenty-five-plus years and fifty-plus years, and a church anniversary service to celebrate the birthday of your congregation. The point: special services raise attendance for that day, especially from members who have become less active. Twenty special services a year raise the attendance for twenty Sundays. Not only is participation boosted on Sundays with special emphases, but many members feel engaged, honored, appreciated, and involved—which inspires them to want to stay connected.

Hold a Fair for Church Groups and Organizations

A fair for church groups and organizations is similar to a boat, home, or travel show at a civic center where, instead, tables line the largest room in the church (fellowship hall?) to feature a table for every group and organization in the congregation. Each offers a person representing that group or organization with information on the table about the group. There might be a table for the choir and musical groups, youth group, deacons, trustees, missions committee, social justice group, adult Bible study, adult education, Christian education teachers, mission trips, service groups, men's and women's groups, and every church group you can think of. The purpose is to provide information and to solicit interest from potential members.

This is an opportunity for members to learn about all the different groups in their church without having to make a commitment to any. Instruct the people at tables not to pressure onlookers. Simply provide a sign-up sheet on each table for fairgoers to express their interest and invite follow-up. Food should be abundant and easily accessible. On this Sunday attendance will rise because many will want to be present to represent their own group, and other members will have the wonderful opportunity to consider how they might become more fully involved or active in new interests.

Plan Activities Involving Children

Any activity that involves children brings parents and relatives. Why? Because children do not drive. Often when children are involved in a play, skit, or musical number in the worship service, the wider family attends. The parent who does not usually attend worship comes for that Sunday as do brothers and sisters, grandparents, and sometimes neighbors. One church with a weekly "Time with the Children" in the worship service, usually by the pastor, substitutes the youth choir singing once a month. Some churches have added a September "Blessing of the Backpacks" where children and youth all bring their backpacks to worship to have them blessed, which, of course, is really a blessing of the ones who are carrying the backpacks and a blessing of their minds, which will grow from what is carried inside the backpacks. On that Sunday each year, the sanctuary is filled with children, youth, and their families for a fun yet sacred acknowledgment of the value of education. Many congregations present Bibles to children, often in the third grade. Couple that Sunday with a breakfast for the extended families (especially grandparents) of the children receiving Bibles and watch the attendance soar on that Sunday.

To attract young families, feature the children in announcements, skits, singing, and readings. Older children are fully capable of serving regularly as lay readers to offer a call to worship, invocation, or responsive reading. Imagine the impact when children look up to see someone their age leading worship. They identify with that age group. They feel included. Imagine a visiting young family with children who see others their age actively participating. Use children as ushers or greeters. The children themselves will feel more a part of the church's life, and their families will likely be in full attendance that day.

When surveys and focus groups ask recent new members and attenders which factors influenced them to come to church, the educational program for children and youth topped the charts. The Christian education program brought them in, but can it hold on to them? Even knowing that education for children is one of the top draws for new, young families, many churches cut that to bare bones when facing financial challenges, and few invest more than they must. What if the programs that attract the most new attenders and participants were worthy of the church's highest investment instead of its least? If meeting the needs of more people in your community truly becomes one of the congregation's highest institutional priorities, dream of the ideal program for children and how it might expand to motivate the children themselves to want to return week after week.

Schedule Work Days and Service Days to Build Attendance

Work days and service days lift attendance and encourage reentry into the worship life of the congregation. Some congregations hold an annual "Day of Service," which begins with morning devotions together, expands out to dozens of volunteer locations in the community, and then regroups for a dinner and video show about the participants. Others have enjoyed holding a "Blue Jeans Sunday" every spring and fall where dozens work on a Sunday afternoon (after a free lunch) to wash the church's windows, polish its floors, repair its broken parts, and clean everything in sight.

Work days and service days build attendance because a group that works or serves together is more likely to regroup to worship together. They provide opportunities for church leaders and volunteers to invite lapsed members to return ("We could use your help on Sunday") or to invite recent church shoppers and first attenders to "join with me to volunteer in the community on Saturday." *Any* occasion to invite new people or those who have attended less frequently to reengage is a golden opportunity to build participation and to meet the needs of more people. A fringe benefit of work or service days is that they build a sense of community among participants. An *espirit de corps* pervades the atmosphere as they feel "*We* did this together." People working and talking along the way deepen their friendships and bond with others whom they may have seen for years but never really spoke with in much depth. The resulting sense of community is beautiful and powerful. Ironically, you cannot set out to create community. Community is a by-product of collaboration in working, serving, or worshipping together.

Welcome Parents of Preschoolers

If a preschool rents space in your church, ask if the pastor and one leader could welcome parents for five minutes at the beginning of each semester, ideally on a parents' night. If the leader happened to be a church member who also had a child participating in the preschool, so much the better. Often there is a cordial relationship between the preschool head and the church staff. Welcoming parents who bring their children to preschool every weekday is a polite and thoughtful gesture for the pastor and leader. Parents have already set foot inside the facility, which makes them familiar with the territory and comfortable parking and entering the church. Once parents have entered the church and are familiar with the lay of the land, they are more likely to feel comfortable returning for worship than those who have never experienced entering the facility. Parents of preschoolers have young children benefiting from meeting in the church. Perhaps some of the preschool families are ready to bring their children to church school as well.

The pastor's welcome to the parents should be brief, welcoming, warm, and include a low-key invitation to attend worship and bring their children to church school. Do that twice a year every year and a few will come. This practice is so easy and brief, yet surprisingly few church staffs take advantage of this opportunity to engage the lives of people who are prime candidates for having more of their needs met at a location where they already feel comfortable. At the pastor's welcome, hand out to parents brochures for the church school and educational programs as a reminder and a resource.

Affirm and Reinforce "Sender Sources"

"Sender sources" are people who continually bring in the most guests. They invite visitors, introduce church shoppers to the pastor, drive new attenders to church, and tell their neighbors, friends, extended family, social media contacts, and everyone they know about how their church meets their needs. They effectively bring new people in the door. These are the 20 percent who bring in 80 percent of the guests. Affirm them. Thank them. Name them. Celebrate them and share their achievements every chance you have. Lift them up as examples of people who introduce others to a place where their needs can be met, much as the apostle Andrew introduced his brother Peter to Jesus.

Highlight these sender sources as a model for others, for they have already demonstrated their effective and successful results. Invite them to hold an after-worship workshop and lead a panel discussion on how to invite people to worship. When people whom the sender sources have invited join the church, invite the sender sources to stand alongside the pastor and deacons to welcome the new members. Nothing succeeds like success. Building up your sender sources will yield great results.

Make Your Website about Them, Not about You

If someone in your community was searching for a church to attend, where do you think they would turn first? It the old days, it used to be the phone book: the Yellow Pages. Today church searchers go online. Perhaps they do a search for "[Name of town] churches." The churches that pop up first are the ones with websites and Facebook pages. When they view your website, will it be primarily about *you*, or will it be oriented to *them*—to those seeking a church to visit? The obvious message of the website should be an enthusiastic "*YOU are welcome here!*"

Old and faithful stalwarts may wonder, *But isn't the website for us?* Of course it can meet the needs of the regular attenders as well, but the website's primary purpose is to provide information to any who search and to attract those whose spiritual needs can be met by your church. Ask yourself, *Who actually views the website? How often do active members consult it?* The answer is rarely, except perhaps to check a date or information about an event. That information can be available on a member's tab or the church calendar page. Overall, the home page should be oriented to attracting new guests. And so use "you" words to explain how the church can meet the needs of those who search out the website. Use photos that encourage potential attenders to "put themselves in the picture." When they search for the website, what photos will they see? The ice cream social? The rummage sale? The church supper showing longtime and mostly older members? They may appreciate the evidence of a church family that enjoys spending time together, but most visitors will not put themselves in that picture.

Are there *any* photos of people at worship where their spiritual needs are met? Are there photos of students and teachers in the education program for those who desire their children to be exposed to role models and values of people of faith? Are there photos of new attenders finding small groups with interests with which they can connect? Are there photos of people who look like them? Or do they mostly look like a different generation or a collection of longtime friends whose circles will be difficult to enter? A picture is worth a thousand words, so make every picture count as you promote your desire to meet people's spiritual needs—people of many ages and abilities, of different races and genders. Be careful here to select photos so that they represent a realistic makeup of the congregation by age, gender, race, and other characteristics. The problem with photos is that most of the photos taken are of social or recreational events, which is not bad at all, but rarely are photos included of the key elements of worship, teaching, and learning. Encourage your members who take photos to try to capture the heart and soul of a congregation worshipping God, learning about faith, and serving God's children.

Your church's website will rank second or third for the purpose of introducing new people to your congregation. Only personal invitations by members and the pastor's efforts will rank higher. The website should be among the highest and most important priorities for a church to implement and sustain. Keep it fresh. Add new photos constantly. Make it easy to navigate, especially for those searching for your congregation. Most of all, keep it about *them*. Not about you.

Form a Chat Group

Establish a chat group among the members on the church's email list. This is a group page where anyone can post anything they like: information about a coming event, thoughts about an issue, links to interesting websites, or recommendations for a new book. It is like a Facebook page except it is limited to members in the email group, which anyone can join. Pastors can post a chat early in the week to tell about the coming Sunday's worship service, the sermon topic, special parts of the service, hymns that will be sung, or any information to encourage and build attendance. Christian education and music staff can post notes about coming themes or music notes about composers.

When members see the chat posting in their email, they will be reminded that their presence is desired at the next worship service, to which they should come expecting an encounter with God. If every chat message from the staff raises attendance by even two or three, it is worth the small effort. Using a chat group builds weekly attendance. Once, twice, or more during the week, the worship service is anticipated and told about via chat. Participants start to think about it, anticipate it, and even look forward to it.

Perhaps chat participants will read in advance the Scriptures that are offered (it is best if they are printed right in the chat message). If there are books or resources that serve as background to the service, they are directed to them with easy links to connect and review. They may start to hum to themselves during the week beloved hymns or anthems that will be offered in the coming week. Parents are reminded anew about the value of their children attending church school. Some members who feel alone or alienated will feel connected, if only by this network of members who hold in common their desire to form a community together. Forming a chat group is technologically easy with big results. Where else can you build attendance so effectively with such minor effort?

Initiate a Sermon Talkback

Add a sermon talkback or other educational or informational programs immediately following the worship service a couple times a month, and especially invite guests to remain. Not everyone feels comfortable going to coffee hour in the fellowship hall, and some may find it awkward especially when they do not know many people and stand alone with no one to converse with. The ones who do not feel comfortable going to coffee hour may enjoy a more intellectually stimulating conversation in which they do not have to know people. Of course it is possible to do both—to pick up some refreshments, say hello to friends, and then come into the program.

A sermon talkback is typically led by the pastor, and participants are welcomed to ask questions, make comments, share their thoughts, or discuss with others. The pastor takes care not to speak much or even to answer questions but invites others to suggest answers to questions raised. The sermon talkback reinforces the pastor's message and aids worshippers to better remember and apply helpful points.

Sometimes a participant's question will throw the discussion completely off topic to something she or he wants to discuss. If the pastor senses there is interest in the group, what can going off topic hurt? Allowing the conversation to continue for a bit serves as a pressure release valve for the congregation, for they know there will be a regular time to converse as a group with the pastor— preferably about the morning's sermon but also about any other pressing interests, questions, or concerns. For instance, participants may want help framing current news stories in terms of their faith and their church's teachings. Where else can they bring those questions on a weekly or monthly basis? Be careful not to present the pastor as the answer giver but as the facilitator of the conversation to help all express themselves and provide suggested answers. The pastor, of course, is well-equipped to add biblical and theological context to everyday questions. The pastor may also find the sermon talkback one of the most stimulating parts of her or his week and ministry.

Create an Associate Membership Category

For those who are not likely to become full members, create an associate membership category. This meets the needs of those who live in two places or who go away for a season every year, college and graduate students, early career people likely to be in transition, and those who do not want to give up their membership in another congregation but who also desire to have more than a casual connection to your church. It costs nothing to add a simple category like this, and the advantage of associate members is that they then feel like they belong: they are insiders rather than visitors, guests, or outsiders. In reporting membership, then, the count might look like this: "Members, 190; associate members, 35. Total members, 225."

Expect high turnover for associate members. No problem. If your church resides in a university or military community, associate members will join for a while and then move on, replaced by others. Some who go south for the winter or north for the summer can connect with two congregations. If their home church is on the other end, make them feel a part of your church by allowing them to be recognized as associate members. Retired folks who downsize and move to be closer to children or grandchildren may have a lifelong membership with their home church that they never want to relinquish, even though the chances of them returning are slim. Allowing them to become associate members makes them feel connected and a full part of the community of faith.

It is not uncommon for associate members to convert their status to full membership in due time. But remember: emphasize attendance more than membership. So why then add another classification of membership? It is not because you want to list more members but because you want to cater to the feelings and needs of those who desire to associate with your church but have reasons to not yet become full members.

Honor Volunteers

Affirm, name, recognize, reward, and lift up volunteers in the worship service and in publications. List people's names: teachers, choir members, cooks, bakers, care team members, liturgists, greeters, ushers, acolytes, musicians, committee members, and so on. Consider the positive impact on a visitor reviewing the bulletin and seeing the name of someone he or she recognizes or knows. That would be a connection, an affirmation, and a built-in witness that this is a church that appeals to someone they know. Naming people frequently does no harm, and no one tires of seeing his or her name in print. On the flip side, imagine giving generously of your time, resources, wisdom, and energy and never seeing your name recognized. That does not lift up. Use every opportunity you can to name people.

Consider Shortening Your Worship Service Length

Long services have the potential to be a turnoff to guests. Where the tradition of the church is to exceed an hour for the worship service, state so in the bulletin. Perhaps at the top of the worship bulletin where the date of the service is listed, a time may also be offered such as 10:00 a.m. to 11:30 a.m., so that guests will know to expect a ninety-minute service.

Contain the announcements where possible. Consider asking announcers not to duplicate announcements that are already listed in another venue, such as the worship bulletin, newsletter, posters, or website. Ask announcers to limit their announcement to no longer than thirty seconds. Limit public announcements to no more than once, rather than telling about the chili cook-off for four consecutive Sundays. Publicize in advance that there will be no verbal announcements on major holy days such as Christmas, Easter, Thanksgiving, and Pentecost.

For services containing added features, consider limiting the length of music. On those Sundays, ask the music director to favor brief anthems and musical pieces. Select a couple verses of each hymn instead of singing all of the verses. Make it up to musicians by planning future services that feature a lot of music.

Use Laity in the Worship Service

If you say in your bulletin that "all members are ministers" and tout the value of a shared ministry, let that conviction shine in the pulpit as participants view their friends and fellow members as worship leaders. If the only people allowed to participate in worship are staff or ordained clergy, it suggests that this is a high church where laity can serve in some roles but are prohibited in others. In contrast, high lay involvement projects the importance of members in leading nearly every aspect of the church.

When the pastor is on vacation or study leave, consider using members of the congregation to lead worship rather than bringing in a supply preacher. This, too, projects a congregation that is member-led and also a senior pastor who is secure enough in himself or herself to allow others to share the leadership. If your congregation favors using deacons as worship leaders, consider a small shift: allow the deacons to either assume the worship leadership themselves or to recruit another from the congregation to read Scripture or other liturgical parts. Doing so allows a wide array of people, including youth, to be seen leading worship. It also builds attendance because increased involvement leads to increased attendance.

For many the opportunity to serve as a worship leader is a spiritual high point. As they prepare, practice, and anticipate their leadership, they are drawn closer to God by inviting God to speak through them and to use them as God's vehicle in worship leadership. Where it is possible, select voices not usually heard or known rather than the usual leaders. While an email invitation to someone to lead worship is quick, the pastor might want to phone the person instead as an opportunity to visit by telephone, become better acquainted, and cement an ongoing relationship. For the person, it might be the only time in a year when the pastor calls and they have an opportunity to chat. When the congregation views worship leadership from people who normally sit with them in the pews, they value the shared ministry in their church and perhaps also wonder if they will have a turn themselves someday to lead worship.

Increase the Pace of the Worship Service

Use more short parts in the service rather than fewer long parts. Remember, many of the people whose spiritual needs you are attempting to meet do not have an extensive church background. Attention spans today are short. Consider how people get their news, weather, and sports in fast-paced, quick-moving, bite-sized chunks. To be sensitive to this reality, speed up the pace of your service with shorter Scriptures, shorter musical pieces, briefer sermons, and less complicated liturgy. A lot of briefer parts make the service feel like it moves along faster and holds the attention of worshippers. When people feel like the service has held their attention, they also tend to hold a higher appreciation for the speaker or leader. Conversely, if long readings, messages, or musical selections allow their minds to wander or to wish the service would conclude, future attendance can be jeopardized. For those who were on the fence about whether they wanted to attend church that day, a faster-paced service that captures and holds their attention is a checkmark in the positive column.

Feature Miniseries of Sermons

A miniseries of sermons entices worshippers to return so they do not miss a part of the series. Consider a short sermon series on the Sermon on the Mount, the Ten Commandments, the Beatitudes, the four chapters of Philippians, the most beloved psalms, favorite parables from Jesus, or contemporary issues as they relate to our faith in God. A three- or four-part series holds the potential to increase attendance of those who desire to hear all of the parts. Too long a series may lose its impact because of the practical realities that most members do not attend all services.

While a sermon series is not the primary reason for most people to attend church, a series will influence a few to come who might otherwise take the Sunday off. When striving to build attendance, every little influence matters. Growth may not result from one or two large initiatives but from the accumulative impact of many small efforts. Publicize the series in advance to build anticipation. Suggest readings for background information for those who might like to delve deeper into the subject. Provide an insert in each bulletin to contain the verses or an outline of points for worshippers to follow along as a study guide and to take home to review or keep for further reference.

Notice from popular magazines how frequently articles use numbers, such as ten myths, five reasons, three secrets, eight techniques, four tips, and so on. A sermon series can do the same. For example, the four best-loved psalms, seven verses for when you feel anxious, three attitudes to propel you forward, or five important women in Jesus' life. Many verses lend themselves easily to a miniseries. For example: "He has told you, O mortal, what is good; and what does the LORD require of you but to do justice, and to love kindness, and to walk humbly with your God?" (Micah 6:8)—a perfect three-week series.

Talk It Up

The Little League coach hollered encouragement to his young players: "Talk it up out there! Let me hear some chatter!" Of course the players were happy to be playing ball and to be with friends, and they were hoping to make a great catch or hit a home run. But they needed reminding. Regularly. Constantly. Sometimes they focused so intensely on their own role that they forgot that playing together as a team is what makes a winning team. So the coach continued to remind them: "Talk it up out there!"

So, too, with building attendance and meeting needs. Talk it up. Members can easily become preoccupied with their own focus so that they need reminding that *they* are the church and the church functions best when it plays together as a team. To keep up the enthusiasm and a sense of urgency, it is helpful to have a coach or coaches encouraging the team to "talk it up." Build systems and safeguards to keep growing your church a permanent priority. Use reminders in the church bulletin, newsletter, website, posters, and social media to inspire members to tell others about their church and how it meets their needs. Tell about programs and services available to the public. Tell about the warm welcome and the ease of entry. Remind members again and again: "Talk it up out there!"

Create a Guest-Friendly Worship Service

Assume that guests are unchurched. Better to err by over informing than to leave visitors to fumble along, trying to keep up with your time-honored traditions. For example, do not assume guests know the Lord's Prayer. In the bulletin or PowerPoint (if your congregation has gone "green" to reduce paper use), provide the full text, or at least indicate whether to say "debts," "trespasses," or "sins." Assume that first attenders will not know traditional service music, and include the lyrics for the doxology, choral responses, and communion songs, as well as for praise choruses and hymns.

Integrate a brief explanation of religious practices and traditions in simple, clear language. Visitors may have no idea what the "passing of the peace" is, what they are supposed to do, or why they are doing it. (Some of your members may not know either!) So introduce that element of your worship each week with a simple, "Greet one another with a warm handshake or hug, and speak the ancient words of blessing: 'Peace be with you' (or 'God's peace')."

For the weekly Scripture reading, consider printing the text in the bulletin or projecting it on the screen. If your church has pew Bibles, you might refer worshippers to the page number in addition to the book, chapter, and verse. You can also help everyone out by providing user-friendly directions for finding the book of the Bible in relation to other section (for Psalms, "Open your Bible in the middle!" and for the Gospels, "Open your Bible to the middle, and then open the second half of it in the middle again"). Whichever strategy you use, you're giving people the opportunity to follow along as the Scripture is read, thus reinforcing the message.

For special elements of a worship service, provide introductory commentary in the bulletin or from the pulpit about what is going to happen. For a baptism, tell worshippers in advance that they will be invited to respond verbally as a congregation. For a Communion service, consider explaining in a brief paragraph what first attenders might expect: an open table or members only? Walk up to the altar rail or be served in the pew? Consume the elements when served or hold them until prompted? Every once in a while, the pastor or deacons might want to gather some frequent attenders or new members to ask them to evaluate how well the church service meets the needs of new attenders.

Chapter 6
Moderate Investments
Moderate Results

Create a State-of-the-Art Nursery

Want young families? Provide what they need. Next to worship, the nursery is the most important ingredient for attracting young families. "Our lives are on screech," said one young dad. The last thing in the world they want to do is discover a church, only to find themselves sitting in the nursery with their own children instead of attending worship and adult programs. Employing trusted staff for the nursery for Sunday mornings is not expensive. Using paid staff frees parents to attend worship, where they find a quiet hour and fulfill the desire to engage with the congregation rather than do one more hour of child care.

Young parents who become involved in the worship and fellowship life of the congregation are more likely to remain long-term and become leaders. In contrast, attrition is high among parents who end up doing the church's child care. Parents of young children hold high expectations when they are church shopping. They expect the church to have a safe-church policy that is clearly stated and easily accessible (for example, online), including assurance that nursery staff and other children's ministry workers have provided federal and state child abuse clearances.

Many young families favor nurseries that are able to text them quickly if necessary or provide them with electronic signaling devices so that the nursery staff can buzz them if their presence is needed—much like restaurants buzz waiting customers when their table is ready. With buzzers, the parents can relax in worship, comforted by the knowledge that if there is a reason they are needed, they can be easily reached. Consider this idea for marketing your church: Market the buzzers! Advertise that your church has a professionally staffed nursery with electronic signaling devices available to all parents. Little things like that stand out in a big way and are remembered: you are the church in town with the electronic buzzers. A message like that also signals parents that the church is serious about welcoming them and meeting their needs.

Because a state-of-the-art nursery is one of the very top draws to growing your church and building attendance, consider a plan to maximize its attractiveness. Paint the walls with fresh and bright colors with decorations appealing to young families. Throw away all old, dated, or broken toys. Create signs at every entry point into the church so parents (and grandparents!) will know where to go. An exterior sandwich-board sign or temporary banner hung outside on Sunday morning that signals the nursery is ready will be an additional welcome for guests with young children. Consider printing a brief, simple brochure about the nursery featuring the paid staff (include their photos), the ability to text parents if needed or the use of electronic buzzers, and easy instructions for parents coming to the nursery for the first time. Your nursery is one of the key entries into the life of your congregation for young families, so consider it a worthy investment of resources and promotion.

Build Testimony Time into Your Worship Services

Find a regular pattern, perhaps once a month, perhaps just before the offertory, where you recruit a person to tell about "How this church meets my needs." Provide this person with direction to speak to that topic specifically. This isn't an opportunity to talk about how busy the church is, how full the parking lot is, or how great the music was last Easter. This is not about how the church has met the needs of a friend, spouse, child, or parent. The person testifying should speak about how the church meets *his or her own* needs. "I was lonely and the choir became a second family to me—plus the director taught me how to read music and sing harmony! I've always wanted to learn." "The preaching really meets my needs in a practical way because it isn't only biblical and inspiring, but it gives me handles for how to act out my faith at home and on the job too! The pastor's last sermon series was right on time, helping me to deal with a challenging colleague at work." "The deacons check in on me if I miss two or more Sundays in a row. They know I travel a lot, so I'm probably just away on business. But they call to ask where I went this time and how the trip went." "The youth minister lets me know how often she hears from my son at college, and I feel better with him away from home, knowing he has someone he trusts who is keeping in touch." "The hospitality ministry is such a generous group of people; I'm not much of a cook, but I love serving with them and getting to interact with people I wouldn't normally get to talk with."

Most people cherish hearing the first-person stories of others, even if that other person is a stranger. It makes the service warm and personal. And on a subconscious level, it reinforces the feeling of members and visitors alike that they are in the right place and have made the right choice to attend. A testimony need only take a couple of minutes, but a consistent dose of personal stories affirms to every church participant and member that your church meets needs. That is the key message. After a while, members assimilate it into their souls. No matter what they think their church does not have or cannot do, they will find joy knowing that your church is a place where spiritual needs are met—and that inspires confidence for them to invite others.

It is not enough for staff to tell that the church meets needs. It is not enough for brochures to affirm that spiritual needs are met. The most effective conveyer of that message comes from the people themselves testifying about how this church meets their needs.

One member told his story like this:

God is still speaking, and while I may hear God's Word anywhere, I most often realize it, organize it, and decide what to do about it here at our church. And while God is present wherever several of us are gathered, it is no coincidence that we have gathered here where so many have gathered before. This church is not perfect; it is not idyllic; it is an imperfect human construct with all the optimism, striving, mistakes, and limitations that implies. But it is faithful, and when I walk in and sit down, I am lifted by the faith of this congregation.

Tell about how the church meets intellectual, spiritual, and emotional needs. Make it not all about times of difficulty or problems, although the church does its best work in those times. Be careful not to speak only about a needy time, like after a hospitalization or in a time of difficulty. One member told the pastor, "People are always talking about the church being for those who are hurting. What about those of us who are strong and healthy?" Make it also about encouraging people to learn about their faith, to think, to process, to analyze, and to evaluate. Describe how living a life of faith helps a person to think critically when watching or reading the news. Share about how faith is a component to decision-making, to seeking one's purpose, and to understanding more of God's will.

The church meets needs for times of quiet reflection, study, learning more about the Bible, being inspired by music, and finding fellowship in the company of others. The church meets needs by calling us out of our own little worlds and making us consider how to live, to serve others, to become more generous of spirit, to forgive, and to love. Ongoing testimonies from members will reveal that the church meets a wide range of needs. What can be more convincing to grow the church and build attendance than hearing anew from members how the church meets their needs? The theme: people do not want to belong to a needy organization; they want to belong to an organization that meets needs.

Look Like You Take Your Mission Seriously

An airline CEO observed that if airline fold-down trays appear dirty, passengers might assume that the airline does not maintain the engines well. If guests find bathrooms with overflowing trash cans, empty towel dispensers, chipping paint, and toilets and sinks that date from the antiquities, what impression do you think they will have? Spiff up your appearance: paint the front, renew the entry, and make bathrooms appealing. Look inviting. A shabby-looking church, inside or out, can appear like you do not take your theology seriously, you do not care about your spirituality, or you do not care about guests. If the front of your sanctuary or the entrance to your church appears like something from a war zone, it becomes the opposite of welcoming: it repels. If your church cannot afford to paint the facility, at least paint the parts that show most: the entrance.

Consider the example of a white clapboard church in a rural town with curled-up paint and bare wood peeking through. It looked dilapidated and made you turn your face away. For years leaders obsessed about how the already strained budget could not possibly afford to fix the problem, even though the wood deteriorated with every rain- and snowstorm. Their focus was on the building. Something changed when they caught the vision to reframe the need in terms of wanting to meet people's spiritual needs. They knew from constant testimony that the church met the needs of their people. To reach out to meet more needs, they said, they must take a leap of faith, hold a special needs campaign to raise money for painting the church, and bundle the painting with other strategies to offer what they possessed to people who were searching. The campaign succeeded, also generating lots of attention and publicity outside of the congregation. Church shoppers and toe dippers started to appear. Some remained and attended faithfully. What made the difference? Reframing the opportunity and priority to meet the spiritual needs of more people in their community, more than just preserving their facility.

Make Your First Impression Count

You never get a second chance to make a first impression. Invest in your entrance: attractive furniture, colorful and contemporary banners, and appealing artwork. Eliminate clutter. Especially for potential attenders who do not have a background in church worship, attractive design beckons them to enter. Some congregations have found it helpful to designate a small beautification committee to tend to the beauty of how things look as people enter and move about. With a modest budget or with the support of trustees, the beautification committee can be on constant watch to improve the "face" of the church.

One church with long hallways wondered how to make it more attractive and decided to line the halls with poster-size museum prints of famous impressionist paintings. What does that have to do with the mission of the church? It might be hard to argue, yet many people loved the look and enjoyed being in a place surrounded by classic beauty. The prints also signaled the subtle message that all of life and all of nature is the domain of God's kingdom and not just religious art.

Another church, using discount coupons to make it affordable, filled its hallways and the entrance with canvas-wrapped photo enlargements of church events, youth, music, and worship. Visitors were greeted with images of people smiling, laughing, singing, eating, enjoying the company of one another, worshipping God, and enjoying the fullness of a life of the Spirit. Your first impression can be a beckoning invitation or an aesthetic turnoff. Change the decor every once in a while. Some art museums display only a tenth of their collections. Take a cue from them and rotate the items that make your church's first impression. Do everything you can to welcome everyone into a great worship experience.

Learn and Use One Another's Name

Calling people by their names projects a warm and personal welcome. The Bible tells how God knows us by name: *"But now thus says the LORD, he who created you, O Jacob, he who formed you, O Israel: Do not fear, for I have redeemed you; I have called you by name, you are mine"* (Isaiah 43:1). Call others by their names to demonstrate that you want to know them and to welcome them personally. Many people will tell you that they are not good with names, so do everyone a favor by making name tags a priority.

If you already have name tags for your members, you probably face the same challenge other congregations face: where to store the member name tags and how to get people to wear them. Some churches color-code the name tags so that deacons, other leaders, or members of the welcome committee are easily identified. One congregation found that members were not wearing name tags. When the people were asked why, the reason was simple: the only name tags available had to be pinned onto clothing. Many did not want to poke a hole in their good attire. After making lanyard and clip-on name tags available, the church found that usage increased.

Wanting to learn and call by name your visitors signals a warm and personal interest in them. Design ways for each visitor to create a name tag for the day, until a permanent tag can be made for them.

Where to put the name tag board can be a challenge. If people must go downstairs or to the back of the sanctuary to retrieve their name tags, usage will diminish significantly. Name tags must be available where people enter. If you have multiple entries, you will need to think creatively about your options. Ask regular attenders for their suggestions. Remind people at every service (in the bulletin, on the PowerPoint, or from the pulpit) to wear name tags and tell why: "Because not everyone is quick with names, we want to make it easy for all to know you and call you by name."

Appoint a Volunteer Communications Coordinator

Public relations, like newspaper or radio announcements about suppers or concerts, is free. To be fair, free PR is not highly effective, but neither is it an expense if you can recruit a volunteer to coordinate publicity for the congregation. Press releases keep the church's name before the public in print and online newspapers, on radio, and sometimes on TV. Here is something that works better than printed news releases: phone local editors or news directors with story ideas. Ideas are the fuel for news reporters. They are constantly in search of a good story idea. If you call them with a suggestion, you are not a bother. Rather, you could make their day.

If reporters follow up on only a portion of your called-in ideas, the result may still be an occasional newspaper article with photos.

Do not send photos to a newspaper. Rather, suggest a "photo idea" to editors. They prefer to have their own photographers take the photos. If they use their own photographer, the photo is much more likely to appear and probably in a more prominent part of the paper.

Delineate between *announcements, news,* and *features.* An *announcement,* in the form of a press release, might tell about a concert or public event and describe the *who, what, when, where,* and *why* of the event. An announcement is easy, but low yield. A *news* story, in the form of either a phone call to the media or a press release, tells about a significant news item. For example, opening a church's time capsule is an interesting news event. A *feature* story idea, which is almost always called in to a media person, is an idea for a story that is media-worthy and of interest to a wider range of readers or listeners. For example, your congregation's music director may be engaged in a wide variety of community music events and therefore merit a personality profile in the newspaper. Or perhaps your church's youth have just returned from a mission trip and have a story to tell.

Features stories are worth their weight in gold and are more beneficial than advertising to attract potential attenders. Who has time to do this? Who has the skills to do this? Most likely not the staff. But if you recruit and train a volunteer communications coordinator, that person knows it is her or his job to get publicity for the church. The actual contact with media takes only a phone call. Once the coordinator has established a relationship with media contacts, quick emails or texts can be used to suggest story tips.

How does the communications coordinator uncover good story ideas? By interviewing. She or he should make the rounds regularly with church staff and leaders to ask for suggestions for stories that might be media-worthy. Speak with leaders about what their groups are doing that might be of interest. What if, for example, your pastor is returning from a sabbatical to the Holy Land? Ask your media contact to interview and photograph the pastor for a possible front-page sectional profile. What if a member of the church who is a police officer or firefighter is going to do the children's sermon on Sunday? Invite the newspaper to send a photographer. A picture, even with only a brief caption, is worth a thousand words. What if a group of members are producing a quilt that documents the church's history? Don't send the story as a press release. Call in the story idea and ask the newspaper staff to come photograph it.

Do not overlook radio, especially radio news. If you have a local station nearby, go visit and cultivate a relationship with the news director. Ask how to get the church's news to them. You will discover that writing for radio involves very tight, concise, and active writing. What about television? An old adage says, "If it doesn't wiggle, it's not for TV." A senior high car wash to raise money for a local store that was robbed "wiggles." A teacher talking about a Bible study of the book of Isaiah doesn't. Do you know that local TV news directors will give you a few minutes of time to visit with them and to ask what they recommend for offering news to their program? All newspersons thrive on ideas, and you might just be the answer to their prayers.

Increase Ministries and Programs; Reduce Infrastructure

When ample groups and ministries are available to choose from, two benefits result: first, the church is more attractive to new attenders, and second, attrition is reduced among current participants. Many churches try to get people to attend, hoping that they will become engaged. In actuality, the reverse is key: the engaged will attend, in large part because the engaged have a reason to be connected. Members of a musical group are more likely to attend frequently and are less likely to taper off their attendance. Increase the number of musical groups, even if they are ad hoc or pickup groups that do not require professional staffing. Also more likely to attend frequently are participants in adult education, mission projects like Habitat for Humanity or the local food kitchen, mission trips, discussion groups, men's and women's fellowships, social justice projects, and interest groups ranging from bridge, golf, and travel to helping others with their taxes or fixing up their homes.

Ask yourself: *What kind of group or activity would grab and hold my interest?* Also observe: busy people make time for things they really want to do. Survey people to uncover what would engage them and cause them to participate. (See part 3 for information about gathering data from surveys and focus groups.) When you have an opportunity to speak with recent first attenders or new members, ask them what kinds of groups or activities would interest them. Try this exercise, perhaps with the assistance of a staff member: count the number of infrastructure committees, boards, and task forces that meet on a regular basis to "run the church." Then count the number of programs and ministries that might attract people of all ages, from youth groups to monthly widow/ widower lunches. What if your church set as a goal to feature twice as many groups, programs, and ministries as infrastructure committees? That would be very attractive to church shoppers and would signal that this is a church designed to meet the spiritual needs of people.

Mission Trips Bring in Outsiders

When you plan a mission trip, you suddenly see youth show up whom you did not even know existed. And they bring their friends. Many youth proclaim that a mission trip was one of the high points of life. Some write college essays about a mission trip. Others refine their career choice because of this rare experience. Youth who have fallen away from church school or youth group return to become active and engaged participants. If allowed by the church, many bring friends from school or from their neighborhood on the trip. When they return, there are dinners, celebrations, and recognition in worship services, and a few mission trip participants will emerge as regular attenders. Their parents become more involved, and some of their friends' parents will explore your worship service.

Work with your education, mission, and youth leaders to design a direct connection between mission trips and a return to active participation in worship. There is some risk that mission trips that revolve around a charismatic youth leader will boom during the trip week and bust the day after they return. Therefore, making the mission trip a team effort with numerous adults and staff involved is preferable. Plan intentionally to reengage the youth following their return by inviting them to speak in worship, usher, greet, serve as lay readers, write reports for the newsletter, and sit together in worship on a regular schedule (once a week or once a month). Attrition following mission trips can be high, so pool the wise minds of your leaders to consider how to harness the energy and enthusiasm of their week away into ongoing participation and involvement in the life of the congregation.

Feature Short-Term Adult Education Units

For better or for worse, people today are not likely to make a long-term commitment. A year-long or semester-long course will draw only the regulars. Instead, create a number of varied short-term programs that meet for a limited period of time. For example, the biblical book of Philippians is only four chapters long and lends itself well to a four-week Bible study. But be sure to balance Bible studies with programs related to current events or popular trends. Consider two- or three-part workshops featuring a community leader (mayor, police chief, town doctor, school superintendent) on a topic of local interest. Have one-night programs designed for parents, and provide activities and child care for their young children.

Identify the many people within your congregation who have something to offer as well. Invite members to teach a unit on a book discussion or a book of the Bible, or ask if they would be interested in doing a seminar or training related to their employment. Recruit facilitators or presenters a year in advance to offer short courses for small groups of people, and promote the offerings widely. Offer presentations about science and faith, domestic violence, politics and religion, health, social justice, or other topics of current interest.

Promote your offerings in newspapers and local media to attract new people. Consider appointing a volunteer "dean of adult education" to take the lead, in collaboration with the staff, to recruit teachers and presenters, publish and promote the offerings, arrange for space and setup, and get the troops out. Plan a year in advance so you can begin the program year with a nice array of educational opportunities for adults.

These programs have the benefit of attracting new attenders who want to become assimilated within the congregation and to become a part of a short-term small group. In many congregations, those who frequent the adult classes tend to be the same regulars. The needs of these faithful must be met, but entering their circle of longtime relationships and friendships can be difficult. Short-term education and program units have the benefit of creating a wider range of participants, some for the first time, which makes it easier for them to become a part of the group.

Add Off-Site Worship Services

As you consider the goal to meet the spiritual needs of more people, consider adding worship services at retirement communities, nursing homes, mental health residential facilities, ski resorts, campgrounds, or wherever there may be a need for what you have to offer. Does this build attendance? Yes, if you reframe how you count attendance. If you normally offer one worship service a week and add a regular monthly worship service at a retirement community, then you should count the dozens who come to the added service. Ministry is happening and needs are being met, right? Publish that and celebrate it: "Attendance this week: 155 at the church, 32 at the retirement community. Total attendance this week: 187."

One of the advantages of emphasizing attendance rather than membership is that you can track it easily and count those whose spiritual needs are met both on-site and off-site. Starting off-site worship services has elements of both opportunity and danger. The opportunity: every congregation possesses some members who have the skills and the interest to lead worship. This provides an opportunity on a monthly basis to give members a chance to spread their wings and engage in ministry at a deeper level. Do not neglect youth in this opportunity, for many a youth has entered the ministry because of an opportunity to coordinate and preach at a worship service.

The danger: overinvolving the staff—although the pastor or other staff members may preach on occasion. Make off-site ministry a lay ministry of the congregation. While this is a beautiful expression of the church reaching out to meet the spiritual needs of more people, it could quickly become one more task that drains the staff of their much-needed time and skills. Ideally, recruit a member with coordination skills to organize, plan, direct, and recruit leaders for off-site services.

Offer Off-Site Programs

If many of your people work in a major city nearby, consider holding programs or groups in the city, perhaps at a restaurant, meeting place, or a member's office or conference room. One church met weekly for lunch at a restaurant and held a series of discussions about the Lord's Prayer. Another left the conversation open for topics about challenges that people of faith face in their careers or in the workplace. Another pastor went to the city to meet after work for an hour with members and their friends in a pub. Over time spiritual needs were met and participants considered the group's meeting a high priority on their busy calendars, trying their best not to miss a session. Inviting friends who might not attend worship in a church but who would attend an off-site program conducted by a member of the church's staff became easy.

Help your congregation to evolve a theology of service off-site as well as on-site. The numbers reported then become not how many members the church possesses but how many people have been served by the church's ministry and mission. You might even consider reporting off-site attendance in the weekly bulletin to inform and also to promote how the church carries its ministry and mission into the world.

Create a Church Facebook Page

Create a church Facebook page with a link from the website directly to the Facebook page (and vice versa). The Facebook page is the page that is primarily for members rather than guests. It is like a family album, sharing photos of the highlights of life together in the congregation. While the website is primarily oriented to seekers and potential attenders, the Facebook page is for the family. But does it build attendance? You bet it does.

Consider: in United States congregations, according to the Pew Research Center, the average attendance on any given Sunday is about 40 percent of the members—higher in the South, lower in the North. And so part of the goal is not only to build attendance with new guests but also to build the participation rate from among the members. A Facebook page bursts forth with energy and the fullness of life from within the congregation and attracts less-regular members to become more involved.[1]

Another advantage of the Facebook page is that when people are searching for your church or for churches in your town, *both* the website *and* the Facebook page will appear in their search—reinforcing your outreach. Remember, building attendance is not just about attracting new first-time attenders. It is also about reattracting members and regular attenders to increase their attendance. Church attendance covers a wide range of habits: some attend weekly, some monthly, some irregularly, and some rarely. The hope with technology is to build attendance of those with less-regular attendance to attend more frequently.

Conduct Focus Groups

Gather together small groups of people who have come to your church in the past five years. Include those who are attenders but not members. Do not use focus groups as a means to convert attenders to members, but rather use this information-gathering opportunity to discover what drew these people to your church. These are the successes. They returned after a first visit. Ask them, Why? What are the important ingredients that stimulate them to keep coming?

Here is a truth that most congregations know well: if you feed them, they will come. Order pizza or treat participants to a catered or brought-in lunch (never charge them) for a one-shot after-worship focus group meeting. Tell them your mission: "We know we meet the spiritual needs of people and would like to meet the needs of more people in our community." Ask them what appealed to them, what worked, what they recommend, what needs attention (do not be defensive), and what advice they would give to the leaders and staff of the church. Your goal is to learn what you can use to become more attractive to those seeking to have their needs met. See chapter 10 for guidance on how to conduct a focus group.

Use a Mentoring Program for New Members

To reduce the attrition of those who join, assign each new member a mentor or sponsor. It might be a deacon or any longer-term member who volunteers to shepherd the new member through the first year. Mentors might occasionally sit with the new members in worship, phone them to tell about a coming event, invite them as guests to a church meal or concert, email them with information about adult education, or check in with them when they have been absent for a while. Mentors provide an effective safety net to reduce the number of those who taper off in their attendance or start to fall away from the church.

Caution: mentors may diminish their shepherding over time, so recruit a coordinator of mentors to recruit, supervise, and follow up. The coordinator might send out a monthly email to mentors with ideas and suggestions and hold quarterly report meetings of the mentors, perhaps over refreshments, where mentors can tell about their mentoring experiences and share suggestions for effective strategies to reduce attrition of new members. Once new members start missing worship services, it becomes easier and easier for them to fall away. When new members know there is someone who personally cares about their attendance, they might be more likely to come to church and attend activities.

The key to getting new members involved is *assimilation*— becoming absorbed into the life of the congregation, connected to a small group, or given a job. Mentors ensure that all new members sign up early on to usher, greet, or serve as the reader so that people can get to know them and they can feel integrated into the faith community. Mentors continually introduce their new members around to others of similar age or interest and make sure they do not stand by themselves at fellowship hour with no one to talk to. A well-organized and supervised mentoring program is a high-priority ingredient for building attendance and stemming attrition.

Make Hearing the Service a Pleasure

What if the acoustics or the sound system works against comfortably listening to a service? Of course improved sound systems are expensive, but more expensive is the falling away of guests or members because they simply cannot hear well. A poor sound system may irritate even those with excellent hearing if it is too distorted, loud, or tinny. Longtime members may commit themselves to stay no matter what the faults, but you do not want to provide church shoppers any reason to give your church a negative checkmark.

Sometimes a sound engineer can help you readjust your audio settings, microphones, and speakers to maximize their effectiveness. One church had a decent sound system only to find out that they had bought the cheapest microphones. When they replaced their microphones with high-end ones, the sound improved dramatically. If your sound system is accessible during the worship service without disturbing worshipers (for example, if it is in the back of the meetinghouse), consider forming a sound system crew to monitor the system during the service. That way, if the pastor starts walking around with the wireless microphone during the sermon and feedback occurs, the sound person can quickly adjust the system.

There is nothing inappropriate about taking a minute during an occasional worship service to ask worshippers how they are hearing. Ask them to raise their hands if they are not hearing clearly and comfortably. Ask them to tell you personally if they did not feel comfortable raising their hand in the service, perhaps because they did not want to call attention to their own hearing abilities. By asking you can identify "dead zones" where the speakers are ineffective. If the problem remains consistent, adjusting the speakers or adding additional speakers may solve it. By the polite gesture of asking the congregation how they are hearing, you signal that the church wants to make hearing the service a pleasure for everyone.

Increase Giving to Purposes Outside of Your Church

Growing churches tend to be the most giving churches. Who knows which came first—the chicken or the egg? The giving or the growth?

Whichever came first and prompts the other, there is a direct connection between churches that give and churches that grow. A congregation that desires to reach out to meet the needs of more people is already giving of itself and is likely to be infused with an altruistic spirit and philanthropic behavior. When new attenders learn of a church's generosity to others, it inspires them. Worship participants are satisfied to know that a good portion of their own giving goes to purposes beyond simply sustaining the institution's operation.

Do not give generously just because doing so will grow attendance. Give out of your gratitude to God and your desire to help God's children. However, it sure looks like the more your church gives, the more it seems to grow. After a natural disaster, one church invested weeks raising money for the victims. Children, teens, and adults all took part. Despite their tight annual budget, they generated more than $15,000 in gifts to help those affected by the disaster. They saw through lenses of abundance and their vision inspired generosity and increased participation.

Conversely, an inwardly focused church appears to be less attractive to new attenders. An inwardly focused church tends to be a self-centered church. All the talk is about *our* needs, and the members display little excitement about helping those who are less fortunate. Members and attenders who desire hands-on involvement to "give back" and volunteer their time find few if any outlets. Enthusiasm for volunteering to work in literacy projects, food kitchens, house building, or mission trips is absent.

Compare the inwardly focused church to a congregation bursting with passion to put their faith into action. People bring their checkbooks to church knowing they will have opportunities and choices to help them fulfill their philanthropic interests. Announcements, weekly bulletins, the newsletter, and the website put the church's ministry and mission to others ahead of news about the church's needs or challenges. When the offering plate is passed, there is a cheerfulness about giving because givers know a significant portion of their gift will go to help others.

How can a congregation become transformed from inner-directed to others-directed? Take the leap of faith and begin by declaring that the church will increase the percentage it gives to purposes outside of itself. The members and attenders will follow. When speech changes, attitudes will change, which will lead to behavior changing and a new spirit bursting forth. That spirit will attract others.

Post Banners and Signs

Post banners and signs outside for special occasions to inform and to invite. A colorful banner will proclaim in living color that something special is happening. Capitalize the word *YOU*: "YOU are welcome to come to . . ." (whatever the event is). Keep banners and signs short, simple, and punchy to be read as cars zoom by at 50 mph. People who have driven by the church sign for years without reading it may notice a large, colorful banner. Some banners may be available from your denomination or from church supply vendors. Others can be handmade or created by local printers or online suppliers.

A simple online search yields many opportunities to obtain banners to promote services for Lent, Easter, Pentecost, Advent, and Christmas. Search for "church banners" or "create your own banner" to find dozens of possibilities. Banners are a great way to promote the opening of the program year, often right after Labor Day. A colorful banner will suggest that something special is happening at your church. A banner may be inviting enough to cause those with little or no church background to explore further and to consider attending.

NOTES

1. Pew Research Center, accessed January 16, 2018, www.pewforum.org/religious-landscape-study/attendance-at-religious-services/.

Chapter 7

High-Level Investments
High Results

Add Musical Groups

More than any other single ingredient in a worship service, the addition of a new choir or musical group will not only increase participation among the new members of those groups, but it will also increase attendance in the service. Someone once estimated that each choir member can be credited with 2.5 people attending worship. I'm not sure where they got the .5, but the point is whole: members of choir and musical groups bring in family and friends on a consistent basis. If you want to build attendance, increase the number of people participating through singing or playing instruments. This is why it is crucial to have the director of music in agreement with the goal to meet more needs.

Add choirs, pickup ensembles, string quartets, recorder groups, brass or percussion, and gospel or jazz. For those unable to make a long-term commitment, create short-term opportunities, such as having the youth sing on Missions Sunday, the men sing on Mother's Day, or the women on Father's Day. Collaborate with the Christian education leaders to have the children form singing or performing ensembles from the various age-level classes. Engage these children's groups to sing in worship a few times a year.

Since each musician of every age generally accounts for one or two others attending worship, build the weekly choir to a 1:10 ratio with one person singing for every ten people in the pews. A congregation with one hundred in attendance ought to have ten choir members singing that day. A congregation with three hundred in attendance ought to have thirty choir members singing that day.

If you desire to build your church, nothing will have a greater impact than investing in growing your musical range. The "American Congregations 2015" study reported that generational changes in music tended to make much "traditional church music" unappealing to young adults.[1]

Therefore, over the last quarter century, many congregations have found that implementing more contemporary forms of worship has stimulated growth. If you desire to reach out to meet the needs of more people in your community, you may need to select a wider variety of service music that appeals to the average Joe and Jane on the street. Joe may prefer a wide variety of musical styles and instrumentation. Jane may favor lyrics that relate to the current culture rather than to a world two to three hundred years ago.

Updating your music department is a high-level investment because music may be the most controversial part of a congregation's life. Whatever is selected, some people will not like it. Change comes hard. A partnership with the music director, pastor, and senior leaders is necessary to educate the congregation about the church's desire to meet the needs of a wide range of musical tastes. That may be the most important goal of all: to gently guide the church to desire to meet some of everyone's interests.

Free the Pastor to Work on Building Attendance

If meeting the spiritual needs of more people becomes one of your church's top priorities, then the pastor becomes a most important asset. Think about all of the ingredients to building attendance offered in this book of which the pastor is the key player. The pastor cannot simply add those priorities to an already overloaded list of responsibilities. The church and the pastor will choose which priorities to emphasize. If a new high priority is added, it makes sense that something else most drop down or off the list. Initiate this change in priorities by creating a "do not do" list for the pastor. That does not necessarily mean that the activity itself no longer gets done. Rather, it gets done by someone else so that the pastor is freed to work on building attendance (see "Share the Ministry" on the next page).

Consider New Activities the Pastor Might Offer

This investment involves changes to the pastor's job description, to include new responsibilities that only the pastor can do:

- Coordinate and host a new monthly attendance development group.

- Coordinate staff attention to attendance-building goals, keeping the objectives central and perhaps even building them into annual evaluations.

- Create special Sundays to attract higher attendance.

- Envision and create (or delegate the creation of) new materials for outreach for print and electronic media (for example, new attenders welcome brochure).

- Recruit and coordinate people to offer their testimonies in worship about how the church meets their needs. The pastor knows best the intimate stories of how needs have been met.

- Recruit and supervise a small-groups ministry coordinator.

- Add a weekly electronic group chat message to tell about the coming Sunday and encourage attendance.

- Visit (or coordinate with a staff member to visit) those who tell the pastor they are church shoppers. Wherever possible, it is advantageous for the pastor to visit church shoppers.

- Add a personal handwritten note to and sign each card mailed to those who visited on Sunday.

- Support and provide ideas to the communications coordinator. In media relations the pastor is the long shadow of the congregation. Some of the stories will be about the pastor. Having the pastor recognized in the media provides public attention that is more valuable than advertising. The pastor also knows about plans that are in the works for future activities of the church.

• Create an additional worship service.

• Be out in the community to represent the congregation and to offer a ministry of presence.

• Oversee and be the one who holds together the church's master plan to meet the spiritual needs of new members and to build attendance.

Share the Ministry

Another investment involves reassigning some of the pastor's ongoing responsibilities to others, which should free up the pastor for things listed above. When the pastor has to visit every sick person, do every wedding and funeral, respond personally to each email, make regular house calls, and attend every church meeting, he or she becomes incapable of doing other things. That model does not support church growth. (The church's governing board may need to vote to affirm a revised job description for the pastor.)

• Pastoral care and visitation. Build a care team to make routine visits to nursing homes, shut-ins, and less-serious hospitalizations. If a person's situation turns serious so that only the pastor will do, the pastor will go. Ninety percent of the time, these are visits that another could do so that the pastor is freed to attend to the congregation's highest priorities. An added benefit of freeing up the pastor from routine visits? You increase the participation of church members in a meaningful personal ministry of their own.

• Change expectations about the pastor's attendance at meetings. Many pastors can be out three or more evenings per week for church meetings. But consider: evenings are the prime times for making pastoral visits to those who have recently attended. Evenings are when most working people are home and available. Which do you prefer your pastor to be doing—sitting in committee meetings or making connections with new attenders? The pastor's attendance at one or two meetings may be absolutely necessary. Change the expectations about the others. Encourage other staff members and senior leaders to fill in for the pastor at most committee meetings. Allow the pastor to drop in on a meeting, and suspend the agenda while the pastor makes a report and visits with the committee for fifteen minutes or so. This frees the pastor to be out where his or her presence does the most good—or allows him or her an evening at home, resting after having already attended to those responsibilities.

• Encourage the pastor to make a "do not do" list. Pastors can be their own worst enemies, wanting to do it all. If they spread themselves too thin, fatigue sets in and nothing gets done well. This is why it is advantageous for senior leaders to review the pastor's job description every year or so, perhaps as a part of the pastor's evaluation. Create consensus about the church's and the pastor's highest priorities and give permission for the pastor to put other things on the "do not do" list with the church's blessing and support.

• Create systems for funerals, weddings, and baptisms to free the pastor from initial contact. When an active member dies or wants to get married, usually the pastor is contacted directly. Create standard forms for member baptisms, weddings, and funerals so that the pastor can contact the applicant after receiving initial information. However, when people outside the church want to inquire about a baptism, wedding, or funeral, that inquiry may be directed to the church administrator. For example, churches receive more inquiries about weddings than actually occur because the applicants may choose another church or location. Have the church office handle inquiries related to available dates or whether the church has a center aisle. The office sends out the wedding application along with a booklet detailing the church's practices and policies. Then the pastor reviews the completed application. If the request is approved, the pastor calls the applicants. Allow the pastor the freedom to say yes or no to applications from nonmembers or long-inactive members. The pastor's decision may be based, in part, on how officiating a service might support the goal of growing the church.

Create an Appealing Youth Program

Recruit, train, and supervise the youth leader(s) not only to run the youth groups but also to share the goal of building up a youth group. Become the youth group in town that every teen wants to attend. Consider an interesting dilemma: do you run the youth program for people who think that the youth should (a) be drilled with curriculum objectives and make it like school or (b) is fun, exciting, and interesting to the youth but may be shallow on content? If you build a youth group that is attractive and engaging, it does not necessarily need to be instructive. As increasing numbers of youth participate, they will gain by osmosis some of the values of the church and its leaders, and they will participate in the worship, service, community, and mission of the church.

Involve the youth prominently and regularly in the worship service as readers, ushers, and greeters. Imagine the impression received by a first-time attending family with teens when they witness a teen reading from the pulpit. That broadcasts that this is a church that welcomes, includes, values, and cherishes teens.

Considering the potential for building attendance and also vibrant excitement in the congregation, a strong youth program may be worthy of your church's heightened investment. Your youth program is an entry for the entire family to become involved as their needs are met and their attendance grows. Youth may be highly active for a while and then move on to college or career. However, their parents may become active while the youth are involved and stay long after the youth have moved on.

Because youth leaders and paid youth directors tend to have high turnover, create systems to sustain a strong program over the long-term. A youth advisory board can help to keep the momentum going even if you have short-term changes in leadership. Involve as many parents as possible in active participation, such as accompanying youth on mission trips, work projects, and field trips, and in discussions. If your congregation has too few youth to make for a strong ongoing youth program, collaborate with neighboring congregations. Consider looking beyond your own denomination, for if there is a congregation of similar size in your neighborhood, it might make for an interesting collaboration.

This ingredient to building attendance, an appealing youth program, raises the question: does a currently weak program justify an added investment? That is, if you took a leap of faith to hire a staff person when there are only a few youth now, would that addition of a staff person build up a vibrant youth program? How long might it take before you would know if the investment was worthwhile? Probably about three years. If you do nothing, little is likely to change. If you choose youth as a priority and invest in staffing, you might benefit with a growing attendance by youth, their friends, and their parents. Might it be worth the risk?

Hire a Small-Groups Ministry Coordinator

Two truths: First, small groups are one of the strongest contributors to attendance growth. Second, they require an immense amount of coordination, attention to detail, and follow-up. Skimp on the second truth and the first one falls through. Small groups are essential to growth and health in medium and large churches and must be staffed. Many pastors or education directors have tried to get a small-groups ministry going, only to find that the details and follow-up are too much to add to their already busy workloads. A sustained small-groups ministry essentially becomes number twenty-one on the pastor's top twenty list of priorities. Yet this is an investment with the potential of a big impact and is especially critical for medium- to large-size congregations. When persons, members or not, are attracted to and attached to a small group, they are more likely to attend worship, to return, and to become more involved. Prioritizing the hire of a small-groups ministry coordinator can determine the difference between success and failure.

Because this coordinator interfaces with the pastoral, educational, music, and office staffs, it is best for the job to be a staff position. The staff member need not be ordained but must be skilled at creating, designing, promoting, implementing, and following up with small groups. The staff member's job is not to *do it* but to *make it happen.* Consequently, the staff member should possess talent to recruit and retain volunteer group leaders and to provide support and resources for them. As soon as the staff member stops coordinating and instead starts leading groups, the program is on a failure trajectory because the staff member won't have time for both. What is needed here is someone to run the program and to make it happen.

If you want to grow your church, grow the number and variety of small groups available for the entire range of ages and interests. There are basically two kinds of small groups: *affinity groups* and *generic cell groups.* Affinity groups are built around circumstances or particular interests that participants share in common: widows, singles, parents without partners, grief support, games, travel, study, discussion, community service, hobbies, sports, music, food, field trips, or any other shared interest. Generic cell groups are where people are assigned to a group for a period of time, such as a year or two, coordinated by a facilitator. In some congregations everyone is assigned to a cell group. These groups may meet monthly, share a meal, grow together as people of faith, and look after one another in times of need, illness, hospitalization, or support.

Create a Staff Position for an Attendance Development Director

Consider: No one wakes up every morning wondering *What can my church do to build attendance? How can my congregation meet the spiritual needs of more people in our community?* Others may sometimes ponder those questions, but what if you hired a person whose job it is to be concerned about it and do something to encourage growth? Making this a staff position rather than a volunteer position has advantages. Jobs have a different set of expectations than volunteer positions—stated goals, job description, staff supervision, and evaluation. The director attends staff meetings, is listed with the staff, and has access to office space and staff support. The position might be part-time or full-time.

One church employed a retired executive who became a highly active member of the staff and who agreed to a salary of one dollar per year. Another congregation acknowledged it could not afford a professional salary but paid an honorarium of a few thousand dollars plus budget and expenses sufficient to accomplish the goal. That director frequently took out to lunch those who had visited the church or had the potential to become attenders—with a high success rate. Other churches have used titles like welcome coordinator or membership development director, but hiring staff recognizes the reality that growth in attendance does not happen by itself and current staff cannot make it happen out of their hip pocket.

Creating this new staff position can be a significant investment. Is your goal worth that? Choose big goals, and then do what is necessary to achieve or surpass those goals. The attendance development director might also coordinate training of greeters and ushers—a task that frequently falls by the wayside and goes unfulfilled in many congregations. The greeters and ushers are the face of the church. They are the first ones encountered by first attenders. The warmth of the greeter's welcome undergirds first attenders' feelings about the experience from the first moment the greeter speaks to them. Which would you rather trust this most important experience to: pure chance or luck, untrained volunteers, or a highly prepared, paid staff member?

Start a Second Service

Starting a second service must be done with great care. This field is laden with land mines that could blow up in unexpected ways and places. Attempting to start a second service has divided many a church and backfired on clergy who thought they were doing a good thing. The conventional wisdom is that when your sanctuary is 80 percent filled 80 percent of the time, you are ready to start a second service. Some church vitality experts have considered starting another service as "putting another hook in the water." As Rick Warren says, "the more hooks you have in the water, the more fish you catch."

There are two significant risks. First, you might be surprised at the number of members who do not want another service because they feel it divides their church into multiple congregations. They will not know who is at the other service, and they also fear seeing empty seats and prefer a crowded sanctuary with a need for adding more chairs. Second, another service is a tremendous drain on the clergy, music, educational, and office staff. The question must be raised: Is adding a service (without adding staff) worth spreading current staff thinner? Or might there be more productive uses of their time and resources if the goal is building attendance and meeting the spiritual needs of more people?

If a second service is considered, address questions like these: Should the added service be identical to the main service, which means staff are simply repeating what was done? Should the added service be a different type of service, such as a contemporary worship service or a brief early morning service? Should the added service occur on a different day of the week or at a different time on Sunday? Will the choir be present at both? When will church school be offered? How will you handle fellowship hour? Will there be parking issues, with people arriving as others are leaving?

If the reason for adding a service is to meet the needs of more people and build attendance, research what has worked in other congregations. Appoint delegations of church leaders and members to visit the pastor and leaders of other churches who have recently added an additional service to interview them about their experience. Here is where your denominational executives are helpful: to point you to those congregations and also to provide valuable suggestions for your own decision-making about adding a service. Many of the best-laid plans have drained resources with nothing to show for the efforts. Engage the entire congregation in the conversation about the idea to start a new service early and frequently so they feel they own the decision to proceed. A top-down decision to add a service could lead to a bottom-up rebellion.

Advertise

Advertising can be expensive and ineffective for churches. Nothing surpasses word-of-mouth advertising, which is free. And yet you need not look far to realize that the world believes in the power of advertising. Advertising holds potential to attract attenders. Generally the broader your advertising (for example, to *everyone*), the less effective it is. Simply listing data about your church in any media is not likely to bring in a guest. Paid advertising in newspapers is generally a waste of money and is usually done either because (a) it's always been done this way, or (b) because somebody in the congregation thinks you should. On the other hand, *targeted advertising* to a small segment is less expensive and more likely to yield results. So who might you consider targeting? That depends on the program strengths and core values of your church.

For example, if you are an "open and affirming" congregation or go by a similar title; that is, if you extend an extravagant welcome and hospitality to people who are gay, lesbian, bisexual, transgender, or questioning, then you might find specialized local publications or media venues that could tell about your church to those who read those publications. If you have a first-rate hearing enhancement system, handicap accessibility, and excellent seating for those who use wheelchairs, are there bulletin boards in retirement communities that could tell about your outreach to people with those needs? Is there a way to advertise your attention to older people of faith in retirement centers and nursing homes? Choose wisely and carefully how you spend advertising dollars, but also consider that advertising works for hospitals, museums, theaters, schools, and businesses. If you decide to advertise in local newspapers, stay off the religion pages. In most papers the religion pages list church suppers, fairs, and church events. If your goal is to reach young families or empty nesters, aim for the lifestyle section, features page, or educational section.

Generate a Campaign Feel to Create a Sense of Urgency

While the ideal might be for a church to always be seeking to build attendance and to meet the needs of more people, a campaign contains a burst of anticipation, excitement, and enthusiasm as well as a sense of urgency. Structures are formed to create leaders, captains, task forces, volunteers, planning, organization, report meetings, themes, new materials, and celebrations. An endpoint perhaps three to five years out is in sight. Like a church's financial capital campaign, an attendance building campaign creates a sense of community as members work together toward a common objective to benefit their church and to benefit the people of their community.

To start a campaign, recruit a chair or cochairs to oversee the effort. Form a steering committee and invite key leaders and people who have skills in communicating, training, visiting, and managing people and details. Form task forces as needed to keep the goal of meeting needs and building attendance before the congregation, to train and supervise greeters, to follow up with visitors and church shoppers, to educate members how to invite people in their social circles to church, and to implement many of the strategies provided in this book. Keep an eye toward the future for when the campaign concludes, and consider how the goal can become woven into the fabric of the congregation's mission and welcome.

NOTES

1. David A. Roozen, "American Congregations 2015: Thriving and Surviving," Hartford Institute for Religion Research, accessed January 12, 2018, http://hirr.hartsem.edu/American-Congregations-2015.pdf, 4.

Chapter 8

Base Your Investment on Data

Your church is more likely to grow if it works toward the goal of growing. Every church *says* it wants to grow, but too few do much to transform that hope into reality. Perhaps the difference between churches that pay lip service to building participation, and those that invest themselves in doing so, is found in the motivation. A church that knows it meets needs and feels driven to meet needs of more people in their community will invest time, energy, and resources to build attendance. That church is others-directed, seeing growth for the sake of others.

If you have read this far, you are likely a leader with vision for ministry to those who are seeking and hoping to find a place that meets their spiritual needs. "As a deer longs for flowing streams, so my soul longs for you, O God" (Psalm 42:1). Sadly, this is an era when increasing numbers who possess a spiritual longing are not turning to the institutional church to satisfy their longing. But some are. Some always will. As in Jesus' parable of the sower, some seeds will always take root. Therefore, choose wisely how to invest energy and resources for building attendance.

One of the foundation pillars to growing your church is this: do not trust gut instincts, either yours or those of others. Everybody has opinions about what might work to build attendance. Some may produce results, others not. To base your work of building attendance on opinions is to fly by the seat of your pants. The pilot's judgement is crucial, but without navigational aids, the plane might land at the wrong airport.

So work smarter, not harder. Base your time, energy, and investment on data. Informed judgment is necessary to interpret the data, but it is data that fuels the furnace of decision-making. How do you know you are meeting needs? Which parts of your community of faith are not meeting needs well? How many have not returned because their needs were not met? What were their needs? How could you meet needs better? How can you meet the needs of more people in your community? You cannot please everybody, so which needs should you emphasize meeting? How can you know?

Ask. To gather data for guiding your church's choices about how to invest itself in building attendance, ask how well needs are being met. Fast-food restaurants, oil change providers, cruise lines, hotel franchises, and online retailers do it, and so do most small businesses and many nonprofit organizations: they all survey their users to determine if customer needs are being met. They all solicit feedback on the quality of the service, the enjoyment of products provided, and the cleanliness of the facility. All of this data provides the company information about how to better meet the needs of the customer. Why should the church do less?

Ready. Fire. Aim. Oops, that is not the correct order. Yet that is exactly how some churches conduct efforts to build attendance. They shoot before they aim at the target. Gathering data informs about what the target should be and determines how well the efforts are aimed.

Asking attenders about how well their needs are being met yields a wide range of responses. A few will be negative, critical, and maybe even hurtful. Those feelings exist whether or not you ask about them, so it is better to ask and to know. Consider the ratings for Internet online retailers. With enough product reviews, a pattern emerges, but inevitably even the most excellent products have a few reviewers who give them only one star instead of five.

Likewise, even a church that is outstanding in every way will have a few people who give it poor ratings.

Congregations are made up of saints and sinners. A few who are drawn to a caring congregation may be difficult people. How wonderful it is that churches embrace those with strong, healthy spirits as well as those with many needs. Frequently people who don't like themselves don't like others either. If your congregation is healthy, it will include a few members with negative attitudes. "Those who are well have no need of a physician, but those who are sick" (Matthew 9:12).

Those stuck in a negative place can tend to give negative responses to surveys. So put all responses in context: in surveys, you are seeking patterns. Look for the overall response, not individual ratings. For example, if you are considering a product from an online retailer that has many consumer reviews, you look for the overall rating. If the product has four and a half stars out of five, that is great. Do not be misled by the small minority who rate it poorly. Likewise, if you are considering how the music in your church meets needs, pay attention to the whole. One or two people who hate guitar music should not cause action to eliminate it. Look for patterns.

Pulitzer Prize-winning writer Herbert Bayard Swope said, "I can't give you a sure-fire formula for success, but I can give you a formula for failure: try to please everybody all the time." No church will meet everyone's needs. However, church leaders, more than leaders of other organizations, may be very sensitive to people's ratings, comments, or criticisms. Some may be hypersensitive to an unhealthy degree. One church leader would drop everything to try to resolve any individual's complaint. If one person did not like a sermon, this leader would go to unreasonable lengths to hear that person out and then report each criticism to the pastor. Healthy leaders put criticisms in context and recognize that they cannot please everyone all of the time.

Data is one of the best ways to examine church members' views in context. There is no single best way to collect information, but the commitment to do so undergirds efforts to build attendance and informs decision-making about which needs are being met and which need work. Leaders will decide how to interpret the data and what to do about it. For example, will you lean into your strengths and build on them? Or will you attempt to correct weaknesses so that more needs can be met? In the next three chapters, we will consider three ways to gather information:

1. Congregational survey (chapter 9)

2. Focus groups (chapter 10)

3. Exit information (chapter 11)

Chapter 9

Congregational Survey

Surveying the congregation could be done by the pastor, deacons, an outreach committee, a member development task force, or any other group. The advantages of the pastor taking the survey is that the pastor can (1) do it in the worship service, (2) fashion the questions that the pastor and the staff want to know as they consider how they are meeting needs, and (3) get it done in a timely manner. Left to a committee, developing a survey has the potential to take months. With guidance from this chapter, a pastor can adapt questions and add others to create a survey instrument that will yield results to inform decisions.

A Few Guidelines for Crafting Surveys

• Start with a title. A brief title identifies the work and communicates to readers the nature of the questions. For example, "Congregational Survey" informs people what the survey is and who it is for.

• Include a short introduction. Why are you asking for feedback? How might the results be used? For example, a brief box at the top of the survey might say something like this: "To help me to meet your needs better and to improve my ministry, I would be grateful if you would tell me about your interests and thoughts. Thank you. —Your pastor"

- Keep it simple and as brief as possible but not briefer than it needs to be. If surveys appear long, they discourage people from completing them. If they are too short, people may wonder why they should bother. Generally speaking, one page front and back (whether a half-sheet insert or a full page) is substantial without being cumbersome.

- Use a good amount of white space rather than trying to save paper by crowding the pages. Dense type can be intimidating.

- Place easier questions first. Survey responders then feel like they are making good progress as they work through the questions. If survey takers labor over challenging questions at the beginning, they may not have sufficient time to complete the survey.

- Leave demographic questions (age, gender, income, education, etc.) until the end of the survey. Ask for this kind of identifying information only if you need it.

- Leave a space for "Other Comments" at the end of a questionnaire.

Crafting Your Survey Questions

Make most of the questions quantifiable. Whether you receive dozens or hundreds of surveys returned, you want to do more than just read them. By quantifying responses you can see trends and overall leanings. Rating scales, for example, can be numbered from one to five and then totaled and averaged. Averages safeguard against giving too much weight to a few extreme answers. Suppose, for example, survey takers were asked to rate the length of the pastor's sermons and overall the average was 4.6—a very favorable rating. Even if one or two thought the sermons were dreadfully long, the pastor could rest assured that she or he was meeting well the needs of most listeners in terms of length.

Vary the types of survey questions. You might include some questions that use a *rating scale* from one to five. Clearly identify which end of the scale represents which level of like/dislike, approval or disapproval. (Typically, the higher the number, the higher the approval.) A variation on a rating scale is an *agreement scale*, which provides a statement and invites the respondent to indicate a level of agreement: from highly disagree (1) to highly agree (5).

A few questions might request simple *yes/no* responses, such as, "Are you a member of this church?" Other questions will require *multiple choice* options, providing three or four choices for people to indicate which answer best fits. And where questions suggest a wider array of possible responses, consider a *check mark* or *rank-order listing*, where people can mark all the options that apply or perhaps rank their top three choices.

Open-ended questions, which invite people to answer a question in their own words, provide some of the most useful responses, but they are almost impossible to quantify. When tabulating and summarizing the survey results (often administered by staff), open-ended questions can be grouped together so all similar responses can be seen. Once when asked about music preferences, one response said, "Please, no more Bach!" Another, placed next to the first, pleaded, "Please, nothing but Bach!" Seeing responses like these side by side illustrates for a congregation that questions can lead to a full range of opinions.

Allow for "Don't know" or "Not applicable (N/A)" responses where appropriate. If, for example, you ask a question about an adult education program that only a dozen people attended, give the rest of the congregational respondents a chance to answer "Not applicable."

Invite a key leader or staff member to review your questions and suggest improvements, additions, or deletions. You might also invite one or two other people to help craft some questions. Two minds are better than one, although try to avoid having a committee or board design the questionnaire or wish to control its approval for use.

Consider making the surveys anonymous—or make the provision of a respondent's name optional. Some may want you to know who made the comments they offered. In any case, assure all respondents that their answers will be confidential. Their answers will be combined with many others to learn about overall attitudes. Then honor the trust of confidentiality.

Some Survey Pitfalls to Avoid

- Leading questions, which hint at a "right answer" or influence the person to answer a certain way. For example, "Don't you think the church should include more contemporary music in its service?"

- Double-barrel questions, which ask more than one question in the same statement. Do not put two questions into one. For example, "Do you think we should add a contemporary worship service in the evening, or should we change the time of the morning service to 9:30?"

- Double negatives, which layer two "negating" words (for example, *not, never*, words beginning with *dis-, un-, non-*), producing a positive effect in the meaning of the larger statement. These constructions may lead to a misunderstanding of the question. Prefer questions stated in the positive rather than the negative. For example, "Do you agree with having Communion once a month?" is clearer than "Do you disagree with not having Communion more than once a month?"

- Religious jargon and traditional ecclesiastical terms, which may be unfamiliar to many churchgoers today. Presume you are surveying people who are not familiar with words such as *narthex* or *sacristy*, or *lectionary* or *liturgy*, or even church seasons such as Advent and Lent. Use everyday language. If you do use more "churchy" terms, explain in parentheses. For example: "If a book study were offered during Lent (the six weeks before Easter), would you attend?"

Frequently Asked Questions about Surveys

When and how should the survey be conducted? Best choice: Do it during the worship service. List it as an item in the worship bulletin. Collaborate with the music director to play soft music while people complete the survey. Eight to ten minutes in the service can yield an almost 100 percent response rate compared to a 5–10 percent response rate for mail surveys. Offering the survey during worship to assess the needs of worshippers helps them understand the importance of this information to the pastor and leaders. Note: if you add this item to the worship service, shorten the service elsewhere to compensate for the time. Consider also offering an online survey through websites such as SurveyMonkey or Doodle, but provide an endpoint for collecting the data.

How many responses are needed to provide valid and reliable results? A sample size of more than thirty will yield about the same overall results as hundreds. Therefore a random survey of more than thirty responses is likely to be as reliable and valid as dragging it out for weeks so everyone has a chance to respond.

What do you really want to know? You want to know how well the needs of worshippers are being met. If there are places where needs are not being met, the survey will help you. You may be surprised that needs are not being met as well as everyone thinks. For example, *every* church believes it is a friendly church. What if your survey reveals that the people in the pews think the church has not been so friendly to them? Also focus what you want to know toward building attendance. For example, if you are considering adding an informal Sunday evening service, describe the idea briefly and ask "Would you attend? How regularly? In addition to or in place of the regular service?" If your data suggests that the sample polled would probably not attend, then why initiate the service? If, on the other hand, the poll yields data that suggest that people are highly interested in belonging to small groups, this information can help guide decision-making, investment, and further research.

Do not be sidetracked by someone or a group of people who think that everybody and his or her mother should complete this survey. Its purpose is to provide the pastor (or whoever gives the survey) data about how needs are being met or not being met. It is not designed as a device to allow members to vent, although for those completing the survey it serves that purpose too. Take care not to be swayed to change the purpose of the survey from collecting data to providing a pressure valve for the entire membership. The survey does not need to be repeated in other weeks, left to rot on the back tables of the church, or offered by mail or Internet to anyone who missed church when it was given. Thirty or more respondents is all you need to collect a reliable and valid overview of information.

Who controls the use of the data? Whoever collects the data controls its use. This practice provides the pastor with control to interpret data and to share as desired. It is not intended to be published unless the pastor desires. Selecting parts to interpret rather than overwhelming with statistics works best. Instead of the pastor listening to deacons telling what people do not like about sermons, for example, the pastor is first to know and put the information in context. If numerous survey responses request more contemporary illustrations rather than historical illustrations, the pastor can start working on this without being prodded by an external group. If members want more contemporary music, the pastor can share with the music director to begin working in that direction. The message is received and acted upon.

Consider Special Purpose Surveys

You may discover that your survey prompts others to want to give a survey too. A Christian education survey can aid staff to know how well they are meeting needs and how to meet them better. Music draws a wide range of opinions, sometimes strong opinions, and so a music survey can inform the music director about tastes and preferences. If special purpose surveys are conducted by staff persons, they can turn to their committees for help in crafting the survey, but the survey goes to the staff person in charge because the staff person is the one who wants the information for guidance in planning. Surveys should not be used by boards or committees for evaluative purposes. Data to evaluate staff can be collected in other ways. If special purpose surveys are considered, collaborate with other staff so that too many surveys are not offered in a short time span.

How to Administer and Tabulate the Survey

Invite a trusted staff member, such as the church administrator, to oversee the survey preparation, distribution, collection, and tabulation. This is above and beyond the staff member's normal job description, so be prepared to provide some overtime, compensation time, or perhaps a nice lunch out as your guest to say thank you.

Preparation. Once the survey is in its final form, have it printed in sufficient quantities well in advance. A good model is for it to be inserted in the worship bulletin either as a half page or as a folded page, printed back to back. A different color paper will make it easier to identify and will also serve later as an identifier, as in "the year we did the green surveys."

Provide an ample supply of sharpened pencils in every pew. Place boxes by every door and balcony stairs where people can drop off their surveys, and label them clearly "Congregational Survey" or other appropriate title. It is not appropriate for anyone other than the pastor or the person giving the survey to peek at the responses. You may also ask the ushers to walk the aisles to collect the surveys after the allotted time, also allowing responders to continue working on them if unfinished and to place them in the box by the door as they exit.

If the music director provides soft background music during completion of the surveys, you can ask for the music to end after a certain number of minutes, signaling the end of the allotted time for completion. Also, ask ushers to collect surveys from the boxes (and loose stragglers that may have ended up in pews or on tables) and bring the boxes to the office.

Tabulation. Attend first to tabulating what can be counted. For example, rating scales can be added on a spreadsheet and then electronically totaled, counted, and averaged. Questions will need to be given a one-word tag so each fits at the heading of the survey. For example, if a rating scale invited participants to rate on a one-to-five scale (five is high) how well they liked the length of the worship service, count up all the 1s, 2s, 3s, 4s, and 5s, perhaps like this:

LENGTH	1s	2s	3s	4s	5s
	12	15	35	55	25

You can tabulate from this data that 142 people answered this question. The data can be graphed from the spreadsheet or presented in a number of ways. One of the most helpful is to give the percentage who answered either 4 or 5 (highly rated). In this case, only a slim majority of respondents (56 percent or 55 + 25 divided by 142) rated the length of the service either 4 or 5 (high or very high). How might that be interpreted? It suggests that the service is too long. Generally speaking, a response rate of 80 percent or higher may be considered decisive; significantly less often indicates a vocal minority but an overall lack of consensus. In such cases, the needs of many are not well met.

Open-ended questions and *comments* cannot be tabulated. The survey administrator should read all of the surveys first and then decide if it is worth the hard work needed to type up the comments. It might not be. Simply reading the comments may be sufficient. On the other hand, there is some advantage to having a written record. In that case, the administrator needs to group all the open-ended questions and comments by similarity and then type them up, perhaps organizing them with similar responses. If a few dozen respond with basically the same answer, such as "I like it the way it is," it is sufficient to type that one answer and note the number of people who gave it.

Confidentiality and privacy. Whoever gave the survey owns the survey. The entire box of surveys should be given to the owner after the data is tabulated. Care should be taken to prevent curious eyes from paging through the survey, so do not leave it sitting on an office desk or shelf. Treat the raw data as confidential information.

How to Use Survey Results

Whoever conducts the survey (for example, the pastor) maintains discretion in how to use the results. First and foremost, anyone who cares to go to this much trouble to collect data is going to care about how well he or she is meeting needs. The data's first purpose is to inform the pastor about meeting needs so that appropriate action, if any, can be taken. If a restaurant's survey indicates that the patrons found the tables unclean and the service took too long, the unclean tables or insufficient service could reduce clientele. If a pastor's survey indicates that a wider balance of music selections is wanted, that informs about how to meet needs better. A pastor who chose the same song to open each worship service was told that at least five choir members did not like it. However, a subsequent survey indicated that parishioners loved it. Put feedback in context so that decision-making is based on meeting overall needs.

As you read, study, and pour over results, look for patterns. Look also for connections. What if, for example, you found that heightened attendance was also tied to a sermon series? Worshippers did not want to miss part of the series. What would that tell you about offering a series to build attendance? What if you discovered that a significant number would favor more sermons helping them to sort out and consider social justice issues? What if you learned about worshippers who were bothered by constantly dirty bathrooms with insufficient supplies? (You'd probably take action on that one quickly.)

A survey is not the tail that wags the dog! One survey commented about the pastor, "Stop teaching us and just give us heartwarming stories." Presumably the pastor is not going to stop fulfilling the divine calling to teach as a pastor and teacher, even if one person prefers a superficial greeting-card theology. You cannot please everybody, and you cannot meet every need. Surveys provide overall data to inform your decision-making, not to control you.

Remember that it is better to know. The feelings and opinions that will be expressed are there whether or not you ask for them or know about them. Reading the surveys will hopefully provide you an overview to (a) not take yourself too seriously, (b) recognize that not every need is met all the time, (c) see that some people in your flock are highly opinionated, and (d) acknowledge that overall your congregation rates highly the most important work you do.

Ways to Use the Data

• Share with your key leaders or leader, and discuss appropriate and helpful responses with your staff. Problem with the bathrooms? Imbalance of music styles? Lay readers unpracticed? Greeters and ushers untrained? Classrooms dirty? Youth not participating? Attendance declining? The data provides you individual pieces of information to share and to consider for action.

• Type up in one report your analysis and interpretation of all of the data in summary form. Decide how to make it available to leaders or to the congregation. If appropriate, consider thumbtacking a single report to a bulletin board where anyone can have access to it, but there it stays.

• Publish individual results in church communication venues. For example, a "Did You Know?" brief note in the monthly newsletter may report that 78 percent of survey respondents enjoy singing the old favorites reprinted in the bulletin, 51 percent attend coffee hour, or 22 percent participate in adult education.

• Report to appropriate boards or committees where discussion and possible action may help meet more needs. For example, discuss with the deacons that 51 percent of survey respondents said that your church is friendly and welcoming. Or highlight that 76 percent of people indicated they started attending the church because they were personally invited. Or share that more than half of people who looked at the church's website found it helpful and up-to-date.

• Undergird your self-evaluation with helpful data. This is not the primary purpose of the survey, but if you do a self-evaluation in preparation for your annual staff evaluation, consider supporting it with data you have collected yourself. For example, it does not hurt to report that regarding your preaching, 90 percent found your sermons engaging, 93 percent said they were the perfect length, 87 percent said you related the Bible very well to everyday life, 91 percent said your messages reached a wide spectrum of theological views, 94 percent enjoyed your touches of humor, and 82 percent appreciated an occasional sermon series. Not bad. Not bad at all. No one ever batted a thousand, not even Babe Ruth.

Sample Congregational Survey

The following is an example of a brief congregational survey offered as a bulletin insert and completed during the worship service. Many other questions could be asked or substituted, but this sample provides an example and template to use in crafting your own.

CONGREGATIONAL SURVEY

To help me to meet your needs better and to improve my ministry, I would be grateful if you would tell me about your interests and thoughts. Please place your completed survey in one of the boxes by the door or in the offering plate, or hand it to me. Thank you.
—Your pastor

Please CIRCLE the number that fits your view.

Rate the length of service:

Too long   1   2   3   4   5   Just right

Rate the coordination of message, music, and liturgy (prayers, etc.):

Disjointed   1   2   3   4   5   Well integrated

Evaluate the pastor's preparation for worship:

Slapdash   1   2   3   4   5   Well prepared

Rate the warmth of welcome in service:

Frigid   1   2   3   4   5   Very warm

Rate the quality, appearance, and helpfulness of the bulletin:

Poor   1   2   3   4   5   Excellent

Assess the inclusion and welcome of children and youth in the service:

Not at all   1   2   3   4   5   Fully and consistently

Rate the inclusion of laity in the worship service:

Not at all   1   2   3   4   5   Fully and consistently

Rate the effectiveness of the service in helping you find spiritual renewal:

Not at all	1	2	3	4	5	Every Sunday

Please evaluate the pastor's sermons:

Boring	1	2	3	4	5	Engaging
Too long	1	2	3	4	5	Perfect length
Irrelevant	1	2	3	4	5	Relevant and practical

How do you feel about the following in the pastor's sermons or worship service?

Touches of humor:

Ugh	1	2	3	4	5	Yay

Political, controversial, social justice issues:

Too much	1	2	3	4	5	Need more

Current events and pop culture:

Too much	1	2	3	4	5	Need more

Occasional sermon series:

Dislike	1	2	3	4	5	Enjoy

Overall quality of sermons:

Poor	1	2	3	4	5	Excellent

How well do the sermons meet the needs of our congregation's theological spectrum?

Too conservative	1	2	3	4	5	Too liberal

Please RANK (1–4) your top four reasons for attending church:

___ Worship God

___ Moments of quiet, silence, peace

___ Beauty of sanctuary

___ Sermons from pastor

___ Connect with friends/fellowship

___ Music

___ Youth program

___ Christian education program (K–Adult), teaching, and learning

___ Service, mission, outreach, global perspective

___ Need for spiritual lift, renewal, guidance, strength

___ Habit, raised to attend worship

___ Open and affirming welcome

___ Belonging to something significant

___ Process my thinking from faith perspective

___ Compatibility with my own theology/views

___ Other: _____

___ Other: _____

Hymns you would like to hear more frequently:

Preferred time for Sunday worship service:

___ 9:30 a.m.   ___ 10:00 a.m.   ___ 10:30 a.m.

___ other: _____

If we started an informal Sunday early evening service for families, including plentiful music, would you come?

   Never   1 2 3 4 5 Always

Please comment.

I like it when the pastor . . .

It bothers me when the pastor . . .

I wish the pastor would . . .

Topics or questions I would like the pastor to consider for messages:

Overall, how well are your needs met by our worship services?

Other comments:

Name (Optional): _____

Chapter 10
Focus Groups

Focus groups are basically conversations between a few church leaders and a selected group of participants. The goal is to gather specific information by gathering people to ask about their perceptions, opinions, beliefs, and attitudes toward the church, with an emphasis on building attendance and participation in the ministry.

For example, a focus group might be formed by inviting a dozen people who have been coming to the church for the past two years. Include both members and attenders (people who come regularly but who are not members). Ask these questions:

- What brought you here?
- What keeps you coming?
- How is the church meeting your needs?
- Which of your needs are not being met?
- What would you recommend to church leaders to meet the needs of more people in the community?

You can see the value in knowing this information as a church leader. What's more, focus groups can be used as an occasion for participants to learn from one another as they exchange and build on one another's views and thus experience the information gathering as an enriching encounter.

Advantages of Focus Groups

Here are three benefits of using focus groups:

- Low cost

- Yield results quickly

- Inform decision-making

Focus groups allow leaders to collect information quickly, easily, and inexpensively about specific questions that influence their decision-making. For example, suppose the church is considering starting a recognition of every board or committee in worship, one at a time. One Sunday the educators would be recognized and thanked. Another month the trustees would be recognized and thanked. Then the board of mission. Over a couple of years, a half dozen or more groups would be singled out and featured, with members coming forward to describe why they serve, to witness about their work, and to be thanked by the congregation.

What would you want to know from a focus group of leaders and members to discern whether the idea is a good one or not? Possible questions might include, "If you were recognized, would you bring family, extended family, friends, or neighbors that particular week?" "As a person sitting in the congregation, would you tire of having this extra feature added to a worship service?" "How frequently should such recognitions happen—monthly or quarterly?" The feedback from a focus group may convince leaders that it is a good idea that would build attendance each time it was offered. Or the feedback may suggest it's a nice thought but not something members would value in worship. Proceed with confidence or move on to another idea, based on data that undergirds your decision.

Focus groups can save heartache and reduce conflict in a congregation. For example, suppose you are considering starting an additional worship service. On the surface that sounds pleasant, ambitious, thoughtful, and perhaps worth a try. Beneath the surface there might lie magma that could creep though the tectonic plates to erupt into a volcanic explosion. Many a church has rushed innocently to start a new service based on a few people's instincts only to find that the decision divided the church and caused significant controversy. Focus groups would have prevented this upheaval.

Gathering small groups from the congregation (as well as church shoppers, if possible to find and include) help leaders to take a pulse and glean information about the feelings, attitudes, and thoughts about starting an additional worship service. Flush out what people do not like about it as well as what they favor. Some congregations have rejected an additional service because members feel it might divide their congregation. They would not know who else would be attending church. They would not feel like a unified family. How would they handle coffee hour? Parking? Church school? Other Sunday meetings and programs? On the other hand, what if a congregation had already decided to aim at meeting the needs of more people in their community by adding a second service? How will they reconcile questions of a divided church family with their goal to grow their church?

Focus groups can help church leaders to gauge the intensity and strength of feelings. No surprise: everybody has opinions. But what is their strength? Suppose, for example, that a few suggest making the entry (narthex) to the church more appealing and welcoming. It currently looks a hundred years old with old religious paintings that somebody donated and a cluttered brochure rack with pamphlets that no one takes, and it offers no signs directing visitors to church school classrooms, the nursery, or restrooms.

What if a focus group revealed that a significant portion of longtime members felt strongly that they did not want to make a change? Perhaps the historic setting is comforting to them. Perhaps one of their ancestors donated those old religious paintings. How will that information help decision makers understand the intense feelings those people have toward change? On the other hand, what if a focus group revealed that most did not care one way or the other and a number favored the change? This is a difference between focus groups and surveys: focus groups help gauge how deep and strong people's feelings are.

A by-product of focus groups is that participants bond with one another, learn more about the opinions of others, create new friendships, and help spread the word about the church's desire to grow the church and build attendance. Some participants may find their interest heightened and decide to become enthusiastic leaders for this endeavor.

Disadvantages of Focus Groups

Here are three disadvantages of using focus groups:

- Results cannot be tabulated.
- Results can be influenced.
- Results have limited reliability.

Focus groups are like open-ended questions of a survey. The data they provide cannot be easily tabulated like rank-order or multiple-choice survey questions. Also like open-ended questions, however, focus group responses can be grouped and reported on as factors to consider in decision-making. They simply lack the quantifiable value that allows us to say that "93 percent of the congregation chose B in response to question 4."

Focus group results can be influenced by the moderator, the recorder, or the reporter. The interactions between people, especially those who know one another and may even be friends, are not completely objective. Within the groups themselves, participant responses may be swayed by one or two strong verbal participants or a "weighty" member of the congregation.

Focus groups rely on the trust participants have in those leading the group and the freedom they feel to truly express opinions. Some may reply based upon what they think the moderator wants to hear. Focus groups also risk false results if a consensus is assumed when not every person has spoken. If half the group consists of highly verbal participants offering more than their share of opinions, the others may silently concede even if they do not agree. What's more, because focus groups lack the anonymity of surveys, participants may not feel safe to voice a dissenting opinion, especially if it involves criticism of a key leader. And it can be difficult to assure participants of confidentiality, for any participant or leader may violate confidentiality—even inadvertently.

For all of these reasons, focus groups do not possess the same validity and reliability that surveys do. Many factors can sway opinions, including the makeup of the group. In all cases, the size of the group is not sufficient to provided statistical validity and reliability. Six to ten opinions are not necessarily representative of the whole.

When Should You Use a Focus Group?

Now that we have seen the advantages and disadvantages of using a focus group, we can determine when using a focus group to collect data is most appropriate. Use a focus group in the following circumstances:

- When you are considering the introduction of a new program or service
- When you want to ask questions that cannot easily be asked or answered on a written survey
- When you want to supplement the knowledge gained from written surveys
- When you know or can find someone who is an experienced and skilled group facilitator
- When you have the time, knowledge, and resources to recruit a willing group of participants

Things to Consider When Forming a Focus Group

Recruit a good leader to moderate the group. Your leader will determine the success of your group. Other leaders or staff may participate and assist in the conversation, but one person should be designated as the moderator. The moderator should have the authority to direct the conversation. The leader need not be part of any official board, committee, or task force on growing your church. Qualifications to seek include:

- Experience facilitating groups

- Excellent listening, interpersonal, and communication skills

- Knowledgeable about the subject or can orient himself or herself easily to be familiar with objectives of the focus group's goal

- Can put personal opinions aside to focus on data provided by others

The moderator should paraphrase and summarize long, complex, or ambiguous comments. Doing so demonstrates active listening and clarifies the comment for everyone in the group. Because the moderator holds a position of authority and perceived influence, she or he must remain neutral, refraining from nodding or raising eyebrows, verbally agreeing or disagreeing, or reacting to any comment in a way that could influence further conversation.

Find a recorder. Someone must record the information. In groups, opinions and values can be stated fast, building on others or in contrast to others, and at varying levels of intensity. Make sure people's ideas do not get lost. A recorder should be recruited to write down what is said, much the same way as taking minutes at a meeting. The recorder should not interpret comments as they are made but capture the exact wording as accurately as possible. If necessary the recorder can invite a participant to repeat what he or she said or can repeat back the comment as recorded to see if it is accurately noted.

With participants' consent, the recorder may audio-record the discussion so that he or she might later transcribe selected direct quotes. There are advantages and disadvantages to digitally recording a session: it is a more complete, accurate, and permanent record but takes more time to transcribe and interpret. Some participants may also be microphone-shy and feel less comfortable expressing their opinions if a recorder is running, while others may feel more confident, knowing an accurate representation of their comments is available.

Decide who should be invited. Invite participants either because of similar interests (for example, Christian education) or because they form a representative group of members or attenders. For example, a focus group might consist of people who attend regularly but are not members. Why? Because leaders might be seeking information about what attracts attenders, why they have chosen not to become members, and how their needs are being met. Or perhaps a focus group might consist of an attempt to represent the entire congregation in terms of age, race, gender, educational level, socioeconomic experience, or other factors. Here leaders are attempting to anticipate how the congregation at large feels about a question. If time permits, you might choose to run a number of different groups to include more people and more different kinds of people.

When it comes to the size of a focus group, less is usually more. Half a dozen to a dozen participants (in addition to facilitator, recorder, and the host leaders) makes for a good conversation. If the group is any larger, conversation will not flow as smoothly. Fewer than five or six participants, however, and you risk collecting too little data to be of significance.

Determine when to hold the focus group. Finding a time to do anything extra in a busy church's life can be challenging. Every time slot has advantages and disadvantages. Evenings are good for working people but bad for those who do not like to drive at night. Mornings or afternoons are good for retired members but impossible for those who work during the week. Saturdays may be good for many, except for young parents who are busy with children's sports or other family responsibilities and activities. Perhaps the most obvious is a Sunday before or after worship. The advantage is that people have already committed themselves to the church for that day. The disadvantage is that adding one more thing on that day may be one too many. Many congregations have found that hosting the group as a lunch meeting following the worship service is the best option.

All congregations know this: if you feed them, they will come. Providing wraps, pizza, or a simple soup and sandwich lunch makes it possible for participants to give you the time they were going to spend eating anyway, so it makes it an attractive invitation. The warmth of hospitality creates an atmosphere of rapport and bond building, small talk and fluid conversation before the meeting begins. The Latin words *com panis* mean "with bread," which is where the word *companion* comes from. People who have broken bread together become companions in a common endeavor. You might forget what happens in a meeting, but you are likely to remember a time when you broke bread with another.

An alternative to lunch is to hold a brunch before the worship service, although this risks excluding members of the choir who are rehearsing and church school teachers who are preparing their lessons before service, as well as those who are not good at getting to early morning meetings.

Provide child care to involve young families. Is it not ironic that congregations that desire to appeal to more young families do nothing to make it possible for them to attend? What are young children going to do while their parents or guardians are participating in a focus group? They cannot take care of themselves. They cannot sit silently in the focus group room without distracting attention. Therefore, offer to provide child care for focus group participants or to subsidize parents to arrange for their own child care. The child care providers who tend to children during the worship service may be willing to add an hour or two in order to make it possible for young families to participate in giving the church much-needed and valuable information about how to proceed to meet the needs of more people.

Choose a comfortable location for the focus group. The best location for a focus group is a lounge with easy chairs, much like a living room setting. The worst is an office or conference room. Favor a hospitable room with softer lighting, a comfortable temperature, and attractive furnishings to stimulate conversation. If possible, arrange seating in a circle. Avoid a sterile clinical environment. Create a nonthreatening space to reduce feelings of apprehension, suspicion, or reluctance to converse.

Decide whether staff should be present. If there is any reason to believe that a staff member's presence may inhibit the focus group conversation, then it is better for the staff member not to be present. For example, if the conversation is about music and the music director or committee chair might hold strong opinions or become defensive in an open conversation that could become critical of current practice, why risk inhibiting participants or placing the staff member in an uncomfortable position? Likewise, if the group focuses on the worship service, it might be best not to put the pastor into a conversation where it is felt that the current practice needs to be explained or defended. Polite participants might not feel comfortable expressing negative opinions with staff members present. On the other hand, it is possible that the staff member herself or himself is eager to learn about the opinions and tastes of focus group members as a basis for decision-making. In that case, it is most appropriate for the staff person to be present and equip the moderator in advance with questions and information.

Conducting the Focus Group

Avoid multiple purposes. The goal of the focus group is to gather data about a specific topic, in this case related to growing your church and building attendance. If the conversation veers off on an unrelated topic, it is the moderator's job to bring it back to center upon the goal. A focus group is not a debate, group therapy, staff evaluation, a conflict-resolution or problem-solving session, a promotional opportunity, or an educational program.

Guide the flow of the conversation. Thank people for coming, and as appropriate, allow time for introductions of all participants. Put participants at ease. Remember: few will have been in a focus group before, so they may be nervous about the experience.

Review the purpose of the group, the goals of the meeting, and the expected closing time. Then explain the flow of the conversation—how it will proceed and how the members can contribute. The moderator might also explain his or her role, which is to keep the group focused on the topic and to make sure all have an opportunity to express themselves. You should have already advised any leaders or staff who will be present that the focus should be on the participants; therefore leaders should listen attentively, resisting any temptation to chime in or become defensive if a criticism is raised. The goal is to collect data from a specific group about a specific topic.

Lay out the ground rules. Encourage open participation, and then instruct how to differ with ideas without attacking or criticizing any person (present or not). Agree that the conversation will be a "judgment-free zone." All ideas are welcome, and participants are encouraged to build on the thoughts of others, but no participants are to be judged for expressing themselves or their opinions. Welcome conflicting ideas while seeking unity among the purpose of strengthening the church.

Begin by asking an "easy" opening question. This could be a very general question (for example, "What do you think about . . . ?") or something more specific (for example, "If we were to start an early morning prayer service, how likely is it that you would attend?").

Make sure that all opinions get heard. Before moving on, ask if everyone who has something to say has had the opportunity to express his or her thoughts. After a while, call on those who have not spoken much to ask specifically for their thoughts.

Create the questions. Focus groups are structured around a set of carefully predetermined questions—usually no more than ten—but the discussion is free-flowing. Ideally, participant comments will stimulate and influence the thinking and sharing of others. Some people even find themselves changing their thoughts and opinions during the group. Go in prepared. Write out in advance a list of topics and questions you want to ask. This list will serve as your guide. The suggestions provided previously for surveys will also apply in this context. For example:

Favor open-ended questions rather than questions that elicit a yes or no response.

Avoid leading questions.

Beware of double-barrel questions.

Avoid double negatives.

Prefer questions stated in the positive rather than the negative.

Use everyday language. Avoid jargon.

Place easier questions first.

Leave difficult or sensitive questions until near the end.

Invite others to help craft some questions.

Allow a "Don't Know" or "Not Applicable" response.

Leave demographic questions (age, gender, income, education, etc.) until the end.

Allow conversation to flow rather than conducting a rigid question-and-answer interview.

Possible Phrases to Promote Conversation

What are your thoughts about . . . ?

How would you rate your satisfaction with . . . ?

How well are your needs met with . . . ?

Tell about how your needs might better be met by . . .

What is not going well with . . . ?

What would be ways of attracting new people?

How do new people find out about our church and how well it meets people's needs?

Some people have suggested that one way to improve _____ is to _____. What do you think?

Do you agree with this?

How do you feel about that?

Are there other recommendations that you have or suggestions you would like to make?

What else would you like to say before we wind up?

Can you say more about that?

Can you give an example?

Pat says. . . . How about others of you? What do you think?

If the church were to start . . . would you participate?

What do you think are the top reasons for / needs of / mistakes of / causes of . . . ?

How would you rank the top priorities for . . . ?

If you sensed that a friend or neighbor was ready to consider coming to church, what would you say or do?

How would you invite a friend to visit your church?

How would you feel about bringing a friend with you, including picking up that friend?

What do you think are the obstacles to . . . ?

How do you get your information about . . . ?

Do you prefer this or that?

Suppose you were in charge and could do anything you wanted to do to encourage increased attendance. What would you do?

This is what I hear you saying. Does that seem accurate?

How strongly do you feel about . . . ?

After the Meeting

Have the moderator and leaders present at the focus group debrief to review and discuss what they heard. Invite the recorder to make a preliminary verbal report of what was recorded. If the meeting was recorded, make a transcript. As soon as the recorder's notes are available, ask each team member to review them. Produce a summary of major themes, common themes, and data helpful to inform decision-making. Report conclusions and summary of the focus group to those with need to know: staff and leaders.

How to Use the Data

Recognize that the conclusions of a focus group are neither a scientific study nor do they possess significant statistical validity and reliability. They are used to provide additional information to decision makers about opinions.

For example, if the board of Christian education was considering the addition of a yearlong program aimed at nonmembers, and if a focus group of ten or twelve participants who were nonmembers indicated that they would attend and would be enthusiastic about having that opportunity, that data could influence the decision. If, on the other hand, the participants thought it might be a worthy idea for others but they themselves would not attend, it would be advisable to gather more information before investing time, talent, and resources to produce such a program.

It takes more than one focus group on any one topic to produce valid results—usually it takes three or four. You will know you have conducted enough groups (with the same set of questions) when you are not hearing anything new anymore; that is, when you have reached a point of saturation.

Couple the data from the focus group with other data, such as the results of a survey. If, for example, both sources of information indicated that a wider range of musical selections was desired with some intensity, decision makers could proceed with some confidence to seek ways to initiate that goal. If, on the other hand, both sources of information confirmed that most possessed high levels of satisfaction with the current musical program, then why invest much more effort to change? ("If it isn't broken, don't fix it!")

The pastor and the senior lay leader of the congregation should receive copies of all reports, surveys, and summaries. Trust your paid and volunteer leaders: they stand a little higher on the mountain and can see a bit more of the whole than anyone else. All data is valuable to them as they lead your congregation to grow and to seek ways to increase attendance.

Chapter 11

Exit Information

Some of the most valuable data is the hardest to obtain: opinions of those whose needs were not met. These might include current members or attenders who have stopped attending or church shoppers who attended once or twice and did not return. Not only is this information difficult to obtain, but it has drawbacks.

First, no church can meet every need. Persons considering attending a church may find fewer of their needs met because they are seeking a different size church. Someone who relishes a diverse menu of programs may not find his or her needs met in a small rural church. Another who favors a small, intimate group of people who all know one another well may not find his or her needs met in a large church. A church shopper came once or twice then told the pastor who called that he is looking for a small group to join with people his own age. The small historic church did not have any members his age. There is not much you can do about that.

Second, information provided may be so highly filtered by the person that it is not accurate or helpful. Those who leave because they do not like the worship format may simply use an excuse, such as that they are leaving because their children are too involved with sports activities, not revealing their real reason for leaving.

Third, people may stop attending because of a conflict with another or because they smell conflict within the church. Chances are that they may not tell you that is their reason.

Fourth, some who start coming and then stop may find that they do not want to go to any church. They didn't stop coming because they found another church that meets their needs better; they just stopped going to any church. They have self-selected out. This is an age of "believers not belongers." "Spiritual but not religious" is a fast-growing self-proclaimed category of people who reject participation in the institutional church. All of us in church life continue to experiment with ways to attract them back in, but the culture is like a freight train barreling down the track at high speed, and there are not many programs that buck the trend for the long-term. Never forget the lesson from Jesus' parable of the sower: only about a quarter of the seed fell on fertile ground and took root. Your best efforts will not attract the masses, but they will attract some. Some will always respond. Your job is to sow the seeds. It is up to God to use your planting to bring the harvest.

In light of these cautions, gleaning any data you can from those whose needs were apparently not met can still be helpful. Many of these people will not be interested in providing information, completing surveys, or attending focus groups. They have gone and see little reason to give you their time. The tools to reach them are the same as above (surveys and focus groups), but they must be modified to this particular group. The following are some guidelines to aid you.

Keep it short. A postcard-size survey has a better chance of being completed than a page-long survey. Consider the data that fast food restaurants collect regularly: was the food good, the service courteous, the table prepared, and the bathroom clean? Have you ever received Internet surveys for goods or services that you thought would be brief but they continued on and on? What was your response? Most likely you deleted the survey unfinished and never submitted it. You might be willing to give a survey a minute or two, but not ten.

Zero in on exactly what you need to know. You want to know if the person who stopped coming had needs that you did not meet. Ask, "Is there anything we might have done differently to meet your needs? Is there anything you can tell us to help us improve how we meet the spiritual needs of those who visit?"

Consider using the phone. Recruit a trained interviewer to use a standard and simple set of questions to call the person who stopped attending. The interviewer should introduce himself or herself politely, promise to be brief, and ask if the person would be willing to answer a few questions to help the church improve how it meets the needs of people who have visited. There will be too few cases to provide any standardized information, so there is little harm if the interview becomes more of a conversation about the person and his or her needs. The goal is not to persuade the individual to return; it is to gather data that can be useful to the church. If patterns begin to form after calls to a number of people, this can provide useful information—but understand that some of it might not be an accurate reflection of why people stopped attending. In a sense, these phone calls are like a focus group with one participant.

Consider Internet survey tools. With simple-to-use online survey designs like SurveyMonkey, churches can create simple and fast-to-complete surveys. Judging from the many Internet surveys that we all receive regularly, businesses obviously believe that surveys provide useful information. It is not likely that most churches enjoy the skills of a volunteer capable of producing effective Internet surveys, but a couple of open-ended questions might yield useful information. This is a good reason why collecting information from visitors, including an email address, can be helpful. Perhaps those who stopped coming might answer the following questions with a sentence or two:

"What did you like best about your worship experience?"

"How could the worship experience have met your needs better?"

"What advice would you provide church leaders to better meet the needs of visitors?"

"What might the church do differently that would cause you to return?"

Sometimes only the pastor will do. There may be information people will tell only to the pastor, trusting in the confidence that the pastor can assure. If the reason for not attending is due to a conflict, a person might be willing to share that information with the pastor. If the reason for not returning is the pastor himself or herself, a person might not say so, but if the reason had more to do with the theology, length, or format of the service, then that can be helpful for the pastor to know. If patterns emerge about dissatisfaction with music, education, mission, friendliness, or programs offered, the pastor can collect that data, add it to other data collected, and share it with staff and leaders.

Sometimes a call or visit from the pastor will encourage the person to return. Is taking the time for this worthwhile? Absolutely. Does the pastor have the time to do this? Probably not. But by reprioritizing and putting some things on the pastor's "do not do" list, the pastor can be freed up to use his or her talents and position to make a difference in reaching out to meet the spiritual needs of more people in your community, for God's sake and for theirs.

Postscript

And so, we conclude as we began, with the parable of Jesus from Matthew 13:1-9:

> "Listen! A sower went out to sow. And as he sowed, some seeds fell on the path, and the birds came and ate them up. Other seeds fell on rocky ground, where they did not have much soil, and they sprang up quickly, since they had no depth of soil. But when the sun rose, they were scorched; and since they had no root, they withered away. Other seeds fell among thorns, and the thorns grew up and choked them. Other seeds fell on good soil and brought forth grain, some a hundredfold, some sixty, some thirty. Let anyone with ears listen!". . .

May you use the various strategies, tools, and suggestions in this book to cultivate good soil and to hear what the Spirit says to your church.

About the Author

John Zehring has served United Church of Christ congregations for more than twenty years as senior pastor in Massachusetts (Andover), Rhode Island (Kingston), and Maine (Augusta), and as interim pastor in Massachusetts (Arlington, Harvard). Prior to parish ministry, he served in higher education for more than two decades, primarily in development and institutional advancement. He worked as a dean of students, director of career planning and placement, adjunct professor of public speaking, and as a vice president at a seminary and a college. He is author of more than thirty books and eBooks. He has taught public speaking, creative writing, educational psychology, and church administration. John graduated from Eastern University and holds graduate degrees from Princeton Theological Seminary, Rider University, and the Earlham School of Religion. John and his wife, Donna, live in two places, in central Massachusetts and by the sea in Maine.